NAVIGATING THE TERRAIN OF CHILDHOOD

Navigating the Terrain of Childhood

A Guidebook for Meaningful Parenting

and Heartfelt Discipline

Jack Petrash

Floris Books

First published in 2004 by Nova Institute Press, USA
This edition published in 2009 by Floris Books

The following excerpts have been reprinted by permission:
Hunting for Hope: A Father's Journeys by Scott Russell Sanders.
© 1998 Scott Russell Sanders. Reprinted by permission of Beacon Press.

'On Turning Ten' from *The Art of Drowning* by Billy Collins.
© 1995 Billy Collins. Reprinted by permission of the University of Pittsburgh Press.

Covering Home: Lessons on the Art of Fathering from the Game of Baseball
by Jack Petrash.
© 2000 Jack Petrash. Reprinted by permission of Robins Lane Press,
a division of Gryphon House, Inc.

British CIP Data available

ISBN 978-086315-708-0

Printed in Great Britain
by Athenaeum Press Ltd., Gateshead

TO MY CHILDREN,
JONATHAN, JOSH, AND AVA
AND MY GRANDCHILDREN,
HARRISON AND SIERRA.

Acknowledgments

Many individuals have helped make the publication of *Navigating the Terrain of Childhood* possible.

Many thanks to:

The Helen S. Bader Foundation for funding the research, writing, and publication of this book and for supporting the parenting work of the Nova Institute.

Barbarina Heyerdahl and Bruce Libonn for their faithful and patient manuscript reading and their insightful suggestions.

Megan Scribner for her fine editorial work and encouragement.

Chip Rood at Gryphon House for helping me navigate the terrain of publishing.

My wife, Carol Reynolds Petrash, for her willingness to lend an ear, to read my work before it was ready to be read by others, and most of all for helping to make this parenting journey so sweet.

Contents

INTRODUCTION
Some Reflections on Discipline   11

CHAPTER 1
Coast to Coast — An Overview of the Parenting Journey 15

CHAPTER 2
The East Coast — Birth to Age Six   24

CHAPTER 3
The Heartland of Childhood — The Grade School Years   39

CHAPTER 4
Crossing the Missouri River — Turning Ten and Beyond   54

CHAPTER 5
Travelling in the Wild West — The Teenage Years   71

CHAPTER 6
The Challenge of Driving — Together and Alone   95

CHAPTER 7
Parenting as a Path of Inner Development   104

POSTSCRIPT
Alaska and Hawaii — Parenting the Young Adult   115

NOTES   120

Some Reflections on Discipline

These two words are often used interchangeably, but at their cores, punishment and discipline are worlds apart. Punishment uses the tools of pain, separation, and rejection to enforce outward adherence to a legalistic code; discipline is driven by acceptance. It depends heavily on communication; its aim is wholeness and inward change, of the heart itself.

— JIM LINDSAY, *The Salem Spirit Newsletter*

Few words are as tricky as discipline. For many parents the term is emotionally laden and confusing. It conjures up all sorts of unpleasant memories from the past: images of stern, angry parents, of threats and spankings; memories filled with fear, pain, and distance. These reminiscences come from childhood experiences that were hostile and sometimes ugly. Consequently, a good of number of today's parents steer clear of disciplinary situations and give both discipline and authority a wide berth. These parents trade firmness for understanding and replace family rules and consequences with on-going discussions and negotiations.

If we survey the current parenting literature, books such as *Too Much of a Good Thing: Raising Children of Character in an Indulgent Age, Raising Self-Reliant Children in an Indulgent World,* and *Spoiling Childhood: How Well Meaning Parents Are Giving Children Too Much But Not What They Need,* it is clear that this kinder, gentler approach to parenting yields questionable results. We shy away from discipline because we have seen its shadow but this keeps us from understanding that discipline is much more about guidance than punishment.

There is a small blue book on a shelf in my office that has made the biggest impression on my parenting. It is a copy of *Reflections on Discipline* by John Gardner which I purchased over thirty years ago. The cover is faded and the interior pages are smudged and discoloured from repeated handling. Invariably, I turned to this book whenever my parenting disappointed me. I have read these pages so often over such an extended period of time that its message has influenced my thinking on the deepest level. Many of the basic assumptions in *Navigating the Terrain of Childhood: A Guidebook for Meaningful Parenting and Heartfelt Discipline* can be traced back to this little book. From its pages, I learned early on that effective discipline should always begin with a parent's self-discipline. This simple premise sets the right tone by placing the primary responsibility with us and on our adult behaviour. When parents lead by example, discipline proceeds in a way that works for both parents and children by accentuating guidance and downplaying punishment.

The word discipline has within it the same root as the word 'disciple,' reminding us that as parents we continually need to provide a model for our children to follow. This model is provided by the family patterns and routines that we establish and by the way we act as adults right from the beginning of our children's lives. The fact is that effective discipline begins at an early age long before the first disciplinary situations arise, and always contains a large portion of this essential ingredient — parental self-discipline.

Although effective discipline starts early and ends late, it must always evolve. The way in which we interact with our young children — the kind of parental guidance that establishes good patterns of behaviour with children who are three, four or five — is only minimally effective with school-age children and usually not effective at all with adolescents. Parenting and discipline have to evolve continually on the long journey of childhood.

For discipline to evolve, parents need a sound understanding of child development. All children make their own unique journey across the terrain of childhood. But regardless of their individual paths, they invariably reach certain predictable developmental milestones. These milestones impact significantly on discipline and for this reason any book on the subject should provide parents with a comprehensive understanding of child development so that they are ready for the dramatic but predictable changes that will occur.

A parent's journey through childhood will inevitably be filled with both precious moments and difficult situations. Our sense of success will be determined by our ability to navigate these difficult areas. I like to think of these places as the flashpoints of parenting. These unavoidable challenges will test us in ways that, depending on our response, will either consume us or refine us. If we can see these events in advance as they emerge on the horizon, and anticipate the difficulties they bring, we will be better prepared for parenting's challenges. Numerous conversations with mothers and fathers have convinced me that parents today need a road map to help them know what lies ahead. The purpose of *Navigating the Terrain of Childhood: A Guidebook for Meaningful Parenting and Heartfelt Discipline* is to provide a guide to help parents see that we all travel a common terrain: precarious, challenging, and strikingly beautiful.

CHAPTER ONE

Coast to Coast

An Overview of the Parenting Journey

Receive the child with reverence.
Educate her in love.
Send her forth in freedom.

— RUDOLF STEINER

Inever imagined that I would work in parent education. I had been a teacher for years and found that work rewarding and, what's more, it kept me fairly busy. But a group of mothers at our school had a study group which took up the topic of parenting. During one of their discussions, the focus shifted from their parenting to their children's fathers' parenting. The discussion went downhill rapidly. In the end, they decided that these men needed a talk on parenting and I was the most likely candidate to give that talk.

I was surprised when they asked me to speak about *The Challenges of Fatherhood*. I was even more surprised when sixty fathers attended the talk. Of course, I knew why they were really there. It was neither the title nor the topic that drew them. Many of these men had shown up, in large part, because of the wonderfully persuasive power of the women in their lives. But there were also twenty-five fathers who wanted to continue to meet and came back week after week for a different reason.

These men brought with them a serious approach to their fathering. They came with a willingness to raise questions, speak about their concerns, and talk about parenting. To my surprise, I discovered that the most serious and heartfelt issues that we encountered were commonly shared by most of the dads. These issues that had seemed to us both private and painful turned out to be some of the most basic challenges of fatherhood. When we realized how common our concerns were, the weight of those challenges diminished and our laughter naturally increased.

This sense that there are commonly shared parenting issues has been born out again and again. My work with mothers and fathers has revealed numerous common parenting themes. These themes seem unique and personally challenging to the parents who raise them, but when we hear the same issues and questions raised repeatedly, it is easy to see that these are common situations that we all experience. These are the predictable bumps in the road on the long journey through childhood.

I soon came to see that parenting is really like a cross-country trip. It is an extended journey through markedly different regions, each filled with breathtaking scenery, widely varying terrain, and unexpected mishaps. *Navigating the Terrain of Childhood* uses the metaphor of a trip across the country to describe the different developmental regions that our children will inhabit and to help parents anticipate the challenges that await them. It is designed as a guidebook to keep us from getting lost or sidetracked as we travel from coast to coast.

On the Shores of Time

Let us follow the path of the sun and begin our travels on the eastern edge of the United States near the shores of the Outer Banks, a thin strip of barrier islands several miles from the mainland of North Carolina. In spite of rampant development, the Outer Banks are still wild and enchanting, a place where the elements are strong and overpowering, much like childbirth. It is a place where two worlds meet — the earth with its shifting dunes and blowing sands and the great mysterious sea, a vast, largely unknown world of water and life. This ocean continually rolls onto the shore, sometimes powerfully and sometimes gently, creating an alluring stretch of beach teeming with life. Few places are as beautiful.

A child's birth is much like this shoreline. It has elemental force and mystery. Our children come from a far off place that is even more mysterious than the sea, a realm that is largely unknown to us. When our child is born, as parents, we step out upon fresh sand. Each footprint leaves a singular impression, just as each day in the life of a newborn is distinct and unique.

Eventually, however, we leave the wonder of the shoreline and journey inland for higher ground. The feeling of newness departs and gradually interrupted sleep, repeated feedings, and nappy changes become routine. We move away from the freshness of the ocean and begin our journey west toward the coastal plain. The coastal plain is a beautiful region, as anyone who is fond of estuaries and bays will attest, but this tidewater region is also decidedly moist. This world of swamps and inlets is damp and wet, just the way the world we inhabit with infants seems always to be wet, requiring us continually to change their nappies and their clothing.

After two or three months, this phase of childhood stretches into a continuum of comfortable predictability and we become accustomed to the journey. We establish basic consistent routines for feeding and for nap times and even the piles of laundry begin to seem more manageable. As our children grow, we are able to spend more time out of doors and with other adults. We have done the important early work of establishing a rhythm for each day's events and we gradually emerge from the marsh.

Later, when our children stand and walk or sit in the pushchair or in the car seat, we begin to feel as though we have returned to the land we once knew. We stand on more solid ground as we move from the coastal plane to the source of rivers and head with our young child toward the mountains.

I have always felt that a twelve-to fifteen-month-old is at a perfect stage of development, especially if, like my first son, the child walks a little late. Smiling and peaceable, he made the routine of childhood so pleasant. In fact, I remember thinking that if it were up to me, everything could continue like this for ages. But somewhere in the distance we begin to see the mountains. They loom on the horizon in the west with the first words of defiance, 'No, Papa. My do it,' or 'No, Mama. My want . . .'

The Appalachian Mountains provide the first major bump in the road. These ancient mountains, which are quite small compared with America's other mountain ranges, seem formidable enough when met for the first time. Whether it is during the terrible twos or the trying threes, many of us encounter a rough time with our children in these early years, stretches where progress slows and we seem to be traveling up hill.

Perhaps it is, in part, our experience of the Appalachians that leads us to look for pre-schools and for other adults to help us care for our children. For many parents this is part of the natural progression. When our children are two or three years old, we begin to consider some kind of playgroup or school related programme, such as a parent-toddler class or a nursery, someplace where our children's world can expand and we can have the company of other adults as well as support for our parenting.

With some adjustment to our routine to include the schedule and other minimal demands of these new programmes and relationships, we come through the more challenging mountain passes and begin our descent. Our journey feels easier now and we can relax a little as we move down hill. West of the mountains we enter a different terrain. The hills are gently rolling and the land has continuity and predictability. The rolling hills of Kentucky and Ohio offer us wider vistas and a simpler lifestyle; much the way it is when children start pre-school and parents begin to have an uninterrupted hour or two to themselves. Our children run and climb their way through the open spaces of early childhood and before we know it we are approaching the Mississippi River and the beginning of childhood's second phase.

The Mississippi

With the coming of first grade, we encounter one of the major turning points in childhood, the Mississippi River. In our nation's history and imagination, crossing the Mississippi has always been a significant event. It turns out it is as much a psychological passage as a physical one. The Mississippi itself is not especially wide, particularly in the northern part of the United States. And the land west of the Mississippi does not seem so strikingly different. There are beautiful stretches of prairie on either side of the river and the wonderful mid-western friendliness can be found in Quincy, Illinois, as well as in Davenport, Iowa. Still, west of the Mississippi, we feel that something is different.

It is the same with first grade. I once heard a radio commentator recall how she stood in tears at the bus stop on the day her son started first grade.* Already she could envision how quickly he was growing up. When her husband asked what was wrong, she sobbed, 'Today first grade, tomorrow college.' In response to her tearful reply, her husband gave her a look which seemed to say 'Don't be ridiculous' and calmly stated, 'Today's first grade and tomorrow he'll still be in first grade.' But she was right. Even now, as she reflected on her son graduating from high school, it still seemed like only yesterday that he was entering first grade.

Many parents, particularly mothers, sense the importance of this passage as their children begin elementary school and they linger at the first-grade classroom door or in the car park, trying to savour and hold on to something that will soon be gone.

Outwardly, little changes with the beginning of first grade. Now that many places have full-day nursery, the school day hardly varies from the

---

* Donna D'Amico's commentaries have aired on National Public Radio.

previous year. Even the school work is not so different since the teaching of reading has trickled down into the pre-school. But on an inner level something significant is changing within the children, for they have entered a new phase of childhood.

This new phase can be called The Heartland of Childhood. The love that children feel for parents, grandparents, friends, cousins, pets deepens markedly in this second phase. If children have not learned through pain and loss to be guarded in their affections, they open their hearts at this time in a boundless way. We all recall how much we loved our friends when we were young, that uncontrollable joy when they came to visit, the sheer excitement of staying at their house, and how we felt like brothers and sisters. We had special signals to summon each other and special places to play. We had an emotional bond that was not obscured by cares and responsibility. The childhood terrain of a seven or eight-year-old is simple and uncluttered, like Iowa and South Dakota.

The world of the seven and eight-year-old is like this region of the country in other important ways. There is a breadth and spaciousness to this time of childhood that is unique. Recently, I met with a group of fathers in Michigan and we shared memories from our own childhoods. One of the men recalled how wonderful Saturday mornings were when his father would wake him up and wrestle with him on top of the bed. This man recalled how he would delight in the thought that his father was going to be home all day. As I heard him speak I could remember how wonderfully long all day was when I was seven years old — how slowly time passed. My favourite day of the whole year was the last day of school. No matter how hard I tried on that June day, I could not see the end of summer. That is a memory from the Great Plains of childhood, a place that is expansive with cloudless skies that seem to have no end.

Yet even this seemingly endless region will not go on forever. As we head across the open spaces of South Dakota, we will soon be crossing the Missouri River and from that point on everything will be different.

The Missouri River of Childhood and The Great Change

Before I ever made a trip from coast to coast, I was told that when you cross the Missouri River everything changes. This thought filled me with awe and anticipation, and crossing the Missouri did not disappoint me in the least. I was thrilled to see the hills begin to roll dramatically in western South Dakota and happy to trade the plainness of the Great Plains for the wildness of this new region.

Childhood has its Missouri River somewhere around the age of ten and crossing this juncture is a significant event. It is a time when the innocence of childhood begins to depart, when beliefs in adult infallibility and happily ever after are altered by a stronger glimpse of reality.

These rolling hills of childhood are brought on by an awakening sense of self, with the accompanying side effects of resistance and separation. For children this can be an unsettling time both at home and at school. Fear, loneliness, boredom show up regularly in this region.

For parents this is a critical moment on the parenting journey. If we do not anticipate this rugged but brief stretch of childhood, we can quickly find ourselves in the Badlands, a harsh region of strong contrasts that can overwhelm the faint of heart.

The Badlands is a place that is both severe and strikingly beautiful. For the native Sioux, it is hallowed ground. For parents, it should also be a sacred spot marking the beginning of the second half of childhood, with adolescence looming in the distance, somewhere west of the Black Hills near the Big Horn Mountains.

Each ridge of mountains foreshadows the great change that awaits our children. We are approaching the Rockies, both forbidding and impressive. These magnificent jagged, icy precipices presage the great change of puberty and the Continental Divide beyond which lie the teenage years.

The Rockies

The Rockies mark the beginning of the third and last seven-year phase of childhood. These will be years of great extremes, of black and white, right and wrong, fair and unfair. We will encounter both the sweet smell of spruce forests and body wash and the foul odour of bubbling mud pots and old, sweaty trainers. There will be clear blue mountain days, fields of wildflowers, and night skies full of stars. But there will also be chill winds, sudden storms, and hazardous conditions. As parents of teenagers, we will experience all of these and more.

We should expect the unexpected as we head west across the Rockies into the high school years with dating and driving. Sudden changes in temperature and unseasonable winds are the norm, as are the predictable physical outbursts of Old Faithful and unexpected volcanic eruptions like Mount St Helen. We will encounter vast stretches of desert as well as pronounced seismic activity around the fault lines. And whose fault will it be? Ours! No matter what goes wrong, it will invariably be our fault.

Still, we will press on westward, drawn by the lure of the Pacific Ocean. And when we arrive at the promised land of California (college) we will have brought our children within sight of the destination. Many of us will be weary from the journey, deeply relieved to have made it this far. Like the original prospectors, the forty-niners, we will pay nearly any sum for what we desperately need: to provide our children and ourselves with some degree of independence. Colleges know this. That is the real reason that tuition is so high!

Then, after four years of growing independence and debt, we will stand on the shore of the Pacific Ocean, recalling the sweetness of the day we started out on this journey and all the wonderful sights along the way. Time will have smoothed the rough spots in our memories and ennobled the challenging moments of this journey, and we will feel a bitter-sweet blend of sadness and satisfaction.

We will have guided our children across twenty-one or so long years and through three distinct phases of childhood. Each of these three phases will have had its unique characteristics, challenges, and requirements.

If we have understood the distinct differences between the phases of childhood, it will have helped us immensely in our parenting. We will have seen that not only must children change on this journey, but as parents we must change as well.

CHAPTER TWO

The East Coast

Birth to Age Six

> What is asked of us as parents is sometimes more than we would expect of any person. That is as it should be; for as parents we have been given the wonderful challenge of growing as human beings while at the same time giving the highest service that is possible — to help in the creative process of bringing another human being into the world.
>
> — FRANKLIN KANE, *Parents as People*

I became a teacher and a dad the same year. When I think back to that time, I am struck by how differently I was prepared for the two undertakings. To become a teacher, I majored in education, did a year of practice teaching in the New York City Public Schools, and fulfilled the requirements to receive my degree. Then I went to graduate school to get my Master's in education. In graduate school, I attended seminars, completed reading assignments, wrote research papers, and had numerous thoughtful conversations with my professors and fellow students.

To become a dad, I had hardly any preparation at all. There was just the one single day that I attended a class with a visiting parenting educator. She came to our seminar to speak about child raising. Since my wife was six months pregnant at the time, I listened closely. But I understood so little.

At one point in the seminar, there was a pause for questions and so I asked mine. 'What is the most important thing for parents to provide for a young child?' She looked at me and then answered with one word: 'Rhythm.'

Now I felt really foolish because I didn't get it and I was going to have to ask another question that would show just how little I understood. But for the sake of my unborn child, I was willing to risk sounding really stupid, so I said, 'I don't understand the term "rhythm." Do you mean I am supposed to stand over my child's crib and tap or clap a simple beat?' 'No,' she said smiling, realizing how much I needed remedial education. 'This is not about tapping a beat. What you and your wife have to do is gently create a regularly recurring sequence of events in your child's life.'

This is rhythm — the predictable repetition of everyday activities like feeding and sleeping that help make your child's life peaceful and secure. This is the stability that parents can provide for their children. It is very important in the early years, for it is through this predictable routine that children come to understand the world.

This consistent rhythm is like the sun, the moon and the tides in our child's life, something natural and dependable. Rhythm helps us establish stability and familiarity in the shifting sands of the first months of a child's life. In the beginning, providing this stability takes continuous effort and determination. Sometimes it feels like we are building on sand and that everything that we are striving to establish is being washed away. The littlest thing — heat rash, colic, or a Thanksgiving visit — can disrupt this routine significantly. But with gentle unwavering determination, a semblance of order can still be established from an early age.

This is an essential part of a parent's job description — to establish a climate of quiet and calm for our newborn-because this quiet, protective environment will affect our children's future development. T. Berry Brazelton and Alan Greenspan emphasize this in their book, *The Irreducible Needs of Children*.

> Chaotic environments, in and of themselves, can also affect the way the nervous system operates. In one study, one of us . . . observed babies who were born with excellent capacities to calm down, focus, attend, and regulate but were in chaotic environments. By one month many were very hypersensitive to sound and touch and had poor motor planning and sequencing capacities.[1]

To provide this quiet, protective environment, parents must simplify their lives for the sake of their children. This means that establishing a quiet, predictable lifestyle is the first step in providing for a healthy childhood. It has always seemed fair to me that the expectations we have for our children correspond to similar expectations that we have for ourselves. If we expect our children to be calm and centred, then we must be calm and centred. Discipline begins with parental self-discipline. The peaceful, consistent, close-to-home routine that we establish with regular naps, meals, and bedtimes will help our children to grow up calm and settled.

In the early years of childhood, parents have their first opportunity to provide one of childhood's healthy essentials — repetition. Young children love to experience the same thing over and over. Whether it is their favourite food, their favourite pyjamas, or their favourite story with exactly the same words, familiarity is comforting to a young child.

This predictable, ordered routine is part of the foundation of natural and nurturing discipline. Establishing a regular routine is no more an exertion of will on a child than it is an exertion of will for the rising sun to wake children in the morning or for the coming of spring to draw them outside to play. Rather, the consistent sequence of events will seem like the natural movement of a celestial clock giving order, consistency, and predictability to each day.

However, establishing a consistent routine in a gentle way does not always come naturally. To make this happen, we will need to be engaged from the outset in three distinct ways: actively, emotionally, and thoughtfully. Our active involvement will help us take care of our parental responsibilities in a timely manner. Our emotional connectedness will help form the reassuring bond that provides both shelter and comfort for our children in the midst of family routines. And our thoughtful attention will help us to discern our children's needs and their own natural rhythms and respond to these appropriately.

In addition to this, our ability to moderate our family activities and to base them on a child's need for simplicity can matter most of all. There are many overly stimulating experiences that parents can limit for the sake of their children. Teips to the shopping mall, trips to sporting events, even to restaurants can be set aside or limited for the time being and replaced by more child-appropriate adventures such as outdoor walks in nature and short trips to parks, ponds, and gardens.

Because parenting calls for our best effort, sacrifice is in order. Raising healthy children is important work, and important work always involves sacrifice. For discipline to be both fair and well founded, a parent's self-discipline must always be an integral part of the process.

A Question of Balance

When we take up our work of parenting with a strong sense of responsibility, we become master caregivers — feeding and changing our children continually, holding them, singing to them, and going to them when they cry so that they learn over time to rest assured. In this way, we provide our children with the protection of our sheltering arms so that they come to see that aspects of their new life are predictable and dependable. We establish this familiar routine through our quiet and gentle persistence, through our unfailing effort, day in and day out. Eventually, our children understand that their needs will be met with dependable regularity.

But it is always possible to overdo a good thing. One of the great parenting challenges is to meet our children's needs without making them overly dependent on our presence.

This is a fine line to walk because good parents care and want to be there for their children. But good parents also know that children gradually need to become separate and independent, even in the first stage of childhood. We should not try to solve all our children's problems. When they play or explore, children need to figure some things out for themselves. As my children grew older, I, like all parents, learned to distinguish between their two different cries, the one that let me know I was needed immediately, and the one that signalled that a different response might be in order.

This was particularly true around bedtime. Although our daughter was a good sleeper, there was a time, between the ages of one and a half and two, when she would fuss as she was put down at night. She would call and cry and either my wife or I would go to her — but not right away. We listened, paying careful attention, and slowly lengthened the time before we would go to her. Eventually her cries subsided and after a while she didn't cry at all.

As parents this, too, is part of our work. As our children grow older, they should become increasingly able to wait for their needs to be met. Patience is a capacity that can be developed and strengthened during the first years of childhood. But it is worth noting that it often takes more effort and attention to help our children learn to wait than it does to simply meet their needs. These early lessons make a difference later on.

In a recent article in *The Washington Post*,[2] Laura Sessions Stepp suggested that children who cried repeatedly and were responded to too quickly were more apt to cry easily and less likely to find acceptance with their peers. Children of anxious parents, she cautioned, become anxious children. In this article, the author points out how the immune system of children who grow up on farms is strengthened by the exposure to bacteria. In the same way, she suggests that children who are denied the opportunity to cry are unable to develop a healthy immunity to life's disappointments. With parenting, it is always a question of balance.

Life on the Piedmont

Anyone who is responsible for caring for young children knows how much energy it takes to keep up with their level of activity. Once children start to crawl and walk and run, parents are hard pressed to match their level of energy and determination. Young children seem to be busy all of the time trying to learn to do things for themselves. It is our job to support and encourage this activity, keeping in mind that what we do in the presence of our children provides an example that they can follow.

I often sit with young fathers and ask them to share their favourite memories of their own fathers. They relate stories of following their fathers around, simply watching them work. There are wide-ranging recollections of garages and basements, of fishing poles and toolboxes. But above all, there are memories of what their fathers did.

Even men who, as children, did not have a father around, have distinct, vivid memories connected to doing. One dad had no memories of his own father, but clear memories of his grandfather who lived in the apartment upstairs. As a young boy, this fellow would go upstairs each afternoon and visit his grandfather who would make him a snack. For better or worse, it was the kind of snack that a child never forgets — toasted Wonder Bread and margarine. As this man related his story, he suddenly recalled something he hadn't thought of in twenty-five years — how his grandfather always spread the margarine evenly across the slice of toast with the back of a spoon. Suddenly this young man was in tears. It was as if this memory, filled with all the love that he felt for his grandfather, was deeply connected with this simple act of spreading margarine on toast. This served as a strong reminder that our simplest repeated actions make a tremendous impression on young children.

Imitation — Childhood's Double-Edged Sword

It's rush hour in New York and a young mother is heading home in traffic with her fifteen-month-old daughter in the back seat. Suddenly a car swerves into her lane causing her to hit the brakes. 'JERK!' is her immediate response. Moments later her daughter is heard in the back seat. 'Jerk. Jerk. Jerk.'

In this first phase of childhood, right up to first grade, children acquire so much by imitating what they see and hear. They learn all the nuances of their native language effortlessly — pronunciation, vocabulary, syntax, and more. This learning happens much more efficiently and in a shorter duration of time than it does later in life.

The reason children can imitate so effectively is that they give themselves completely to the world around them. What young children see they become. This capacity for imitation is based on children's selfless devotion and love for their parents. This, of course, has both its positive and negative side.

> When I was a boy, I would sit and wait on the stoop each day for my father to come home from work. I would stand there looking up the street with two baseball gloves and a ball in my hand. The first words out of my mouth were always the same: 'Can we have a catch?' My dad was a refrigeration engineer and a steamfitter, and often his days were physically demanding. I can't ever remember him saying that he was too tired to play. We would stand out on the narrow sidewalk in front of our house on a fairly busy New York City street and throw a ball. I can still see him in my mind standing there as I tried my fancy pitches. He was anticipating my wildness and I never let him down. Invariably, one of my errant throws would evade him and roll into the street where a car or

a bus would hit it and send it farther down the block, a decent walk from where we stood. It was then that my father would give me an exasperated look, a look that seemed to say both 'I knew that you were going to do that' and 'How many times have I told you . . .' Many years later, I was sitting at the kitchen table with my younger son, who was a lot like I was as a child. We were eating lunch and he was playing with his milk when suddenly the glass tipped over and the milk spilled all over the table. The first thing I thought was that I knew he was going to do that, and then, how many times had I told him not to play with his glass. Without saying a word it happened. I gave him the look. I couldn't see my face, but I knew it was the very same look that my dad used to give me. It was mine now. Not because I wanted it, but just because so often what we see as a child we become, like it or not.[3]

Young children love the world without reservation and give themselves fully to each experience. They have no filter between what they see and what they internalize. They can't say to themselves: 'Oh, my dad's not at his best today, I'd better not imitate what he just said,' or 'My mum's a little upset today, I'd better not imitate her.' Instead, young children have an irrepressible urge to mimic what they see others do and that places tremendous responsibility on parents.

We all carry within us exact replicas of our parents' behaviour. This legacy could be something as small as a gesture, the way we turn our head or move our hands. Recently, I was visiting my mother and we were in the car driving on an expressway when we passed a police car parked in a lay-by. I lifted my palms and thumbs slightly from the steering wheel to check my speedometer and my mother commented, 'You just reminded me of your father. He used to lift his hands in the same way when he drove.'

Imitation is a double-edged sword. We can inherit the gift of an irrepressible sense of humour or the ability to stay calm in the midst of crisis, but we can also acquire a predisposition for dishonesty or for uncontrollable anger. These traits come to us at a young age because as children we are ready to receive anything our parents have to offer. This is a wonderful expression of absolute trust. But it can also be painful because so much of what children receive in this way can become their burden for life.

The old adage, 'The sins of the father shall be visited upon the son,' recognizes that imitation has its shadow side. We know that children from families where substance abuse has been a problem are more likely to develop similar dependencies in their lives. We also know that children who have suffered abuse, either physical or sexual, are at a greater risk of becoming abusers. We even know that children of divorce are more likely to have difficulty committing to a long-term relationship. Young people today struggle with these issues, trying hard to prevent the events of the past from becoming the chains of the future.

If as children we were reprimanded with yelling and hitting, this will leave its mark on our parenting. In similar situations with our own children, we will be disturbed to discover that, in spite of pledges to the contrary, we are disposed to do the same thing. Austrian educator, Rudolf Steiner, expressed this understanding years ago in his essay entitled, 'The Education of the Child.'

> Children imitate what happens in their physical environment ... 'Physical environment' must ... be understood in the widest sense imaginable. It includes not just what happens around children ... but everything that can be perceived by their senses, that can work on the inner powers of children. This includes all moral or immoral actions, all wise or foolish actions that children see.[4]

Our responses can be so deeply engrained that they may almost seem genetic and beyond our control. What we learn through imitation at an early age influences us on the deepest level. But in most situations change is still possible. Rectifying the situation may be difficult, but it is not beyond our reach. It will, however, call for an intense commitment, similar to that required in a twelve-step programme, a commitment that must be continually renewed with a daily resolution.

Recognizing the importance of imitation, parents come to a renewed, and at times overwhelming, sense of responsibility, knowing that we need to be at our best for our children. We are obliged to act in a manner that is worthy of imitation because our behaviour will form the foundation upon which our children's behaviour will develop. Our words, our actions, even our facial expressions, will influence them. Our seemingly insignificant behaviours in the kitchen and at the dining-room table will have a lasting impact on their future habits and dispositions.

While what we do in the presence of our children is of the utmost importance, it is who we are as parents that matters most of all. Our convictions — our values and beliefs — will become the unseen bedrock upon which everything rests. Several years ago when my father passed away, I was asked to give the eulogy at his memorial service. I decided to speak about the many things that my father had taught me. But in preparing my remarks, I was surprised to realize that my dad had taught me so much without ever saying a word. The important lessons — like spending time with your family and keeping your word — I had come to understand just by being around him because they were central to who he was and always a part of what he did.

Although this imitative aspect of early childhood can seem like a substantial burden, it is also our greatest asset. It is through this imitative capacity that parents can consciously begin to teach their children important discipline lessons.

Bedtime

For example, bedtime can be one of the more challenging undertakings for today's parents. Trying to move a child from playtime to clean up, from washing up to pyjamas can prove to be a frustrating experience, especially when our children are moving through the Appalachians of childhood. A growing sense of self enables three-year-old children to express their likes and dislikes strongly and stubbornly. At this challenging juncture, a parent needs to keep one important thought in mind: parenting is all about timing.

Imagine a situation that occurs in houses around the country. It's Sunday evening and friends are over. It is the end of a beautiful autumn day with ample sunshine and large amounts of outdoor play. It is a day that seems too nice to hurry indoors and so the dinner preparations are started late.

Having finally finished dinner, the adults linger over coffee and the conversation continues. Watches are checked, the late hour is noted, but it is hard to get up from the table. Although the children are playing nearby, the tell-tale signs that they are growing tired go unnoticed — until there are tears. Then the goodbyes happen quickly.

Once the company is gone, clean up and the bedtime routine commence in a hurry. Toys are hastily gathered up amidst complaining. In the bedroom, the father starts to undress his young son, trying to quickly get him ready for bed. In his rush, the dad is more vigorous than usual and as he removes his son's tight tee shirt, he pulls it too hard over his ears. Immediately the young boy dissolves into tears. Though he has probably had his shirt removed in a similar fashion before, because he is overtired it is more than he can handle. His crying intensifies and everyone is on the verge of 'losing it.'

The old saying, 'He who hesitates is lost,' applies to parenting. It is much better to begin bedtime's preparations five minutes early rather than twenty minutes late. Having a head start helps us to begin the transition to bedtime consciously and fully prepared. If we begin the process when we are still in conversation or behind a newspaper or during a television commercial, we are heading for failure. Good parenting requires undivided attention, the kind of focus we give to important endeavours.

Because young children imitate, parents must be ready to provide a model of how to clean up so that our children can see and imitate the type of behaviour we are expecting. Please understand that this does not mean that we clean up for our children, but rather that by participating in the process with the children, we make the act of cleaning up that much more appealing. In a perfect world we would be like Tom Sawyer whitewashing a fence, making a simple job look like fun.

This will be our same goal when we accompany our child to the bathroom. We must be able to demonstrate the art of washing-up in such a way that it seems compelling and irresistible. The sense of drama that we use when regulating the water pressure coming out of the tap or when squeezing the toothpaste out of its tube is significant. These actions, which speak far louder than words, will show our children just how to run the water so that it doesn't splash all over the floor, how the soap goes back in the soap dish when we are done washing, and how the cap actually goes back on the toothpaste. Everything we do instructs our children. That is why it is so important to demonstrate these things for them each and every day when they are three, four, and five, and then to allow them time to do the same thing carefully themselves.

The same applies when children are getting undressed and ready for bed. All these simple actions become part of the bedtime ritual, a structure that shapes and safeguards the bedtime routine. We help our child take off their shoes and then we both take them to the closet. 'This is where the shoes sleep.' We take the trousers (with the trouser legs right side out) and we place them neatly on a chair, or on a hook, or on a hanger. All is done with an unhurried, ceremonious air, keeping in mind that this is the way it works with imitation and modelling in the first phase of childhood when our children are east of the Mississippi.

The bedtime ceremony continues even when our children are in bed and under the covers. It is then that we begin the transition from being awake to sleeping knowing that this will not happen instantly. Little by little, parents need to bring closure to the day by diminishing the light in the room. The quiet light of a candle or a night-light prepares a child for story and sleep at the same time. A song accompanied by a back rub quiets and soothes a child. And our quiet presence, after a prayer has been said, reassures the child. This is no hasty procedure; it can take a while. Yet, our focused effort is economical. Fifteen minutes of story, prayer, and song, can prevent an hour of 'I'm hungry. I'm scared. I'm thirsty.'

When we look at parenting in this way we see clearly that self-discipline is the key and it is our self-discipline we must develop. We must marshal the strength and determination to actively accompany our children on this first part of their journey from coast to coast. This requires a great investment of time, energy, and focus. For this to be successful we need to commit to a consistently rhythmic routine — daily, weekly, and monthly. In the long run, our self-discipline will be an investment, money in the bank, for there will come a time around the age of six or seven, when our child will say, 'Can I get washed all by myself tonight?' And then we must repress the urge to stand up, pump our fist, and shout an emphatic, 'Yes!' Rather we should conceal our excitement and discretely say, 'Do you know all you have to do? Good. And you'll remember to hang up the towel and put your clothes away? Okay. You go ahead and I will come and see how you're doing.' Then our children will be so proud, like they are when they first ride a two-wheeler. Certainly, the training wheels are still on and we are nearby ready to catch them if they fall, but a new era is about to begin. We are getting ready to cross the Mississippi and our parenting journey is about to enter a new phase.

Road Blocks East of the Mississippi

Before ending this chapter, it should be noted that even with making optimal use of the principle of imitation in the first phase of childhood, there will still be times when our children will resist our modelled behaviour and act in all sorts of unexpected ways. Sometimes all we can do is to ask ourselves if there is any harm in what our child is doing.

A small child who consistently empties a bookcase or repeatedly opens and closes a cabinet door is not really doing anything wrong. They are simply exploring objects, space, and movement. When we have the wherewithal to really look at what they are doing, we can see that this behaviour may be inconvenient, but it is not really bad. In fact, it may be developmentally necessary.

However, there will be other times that our children will do something dangerous. They may run with a glass in their hand or walk toward a busy street. At those times, they will need to be quickly redirected.

Fortunately, little children are eminently easy to distract and often the best way to deter them is to just enthusiastically present them with another option. This approach often works well and is preferable to a battle of wills which generally leads to disaster.

Recently I was in New York having dinner with my cousin. She is a great mum who loves her daughter dearly and is trying hard to establish certain expectations and limits. Her daughter, who is about a year and a half, is a bright little girl, and like bright children everywhere, she could not resist the opportunity to demonstrate her more challenging behaviour for company. While we were finishing our meal, she looked over at her mother and, from her high chair perch, put both her feet up on the table.

My cousin was both surprised by this uncharacteristic behaviour and embarrassed, and she did what most of us have done in similar situations. She removed her daughter's feet from the table and told her, 'No!' Of course, the little feet went right back on the table again and again and again. It is especially in situations like these that parents are wise to redirect and resist a confrontational test of wills.

According to Ellyn Satter, in her book *How to Get Your Kid to Eat But Not Too Much*, a study showed that the average toddler needs to be redirected on average about nine times an hour. Over the course of a day, that's a lot of redirecting. What's a parent to do? It is in situations like these that creative parenting is needed. Satter goes on to tell the story of her son.

> At age two, Curtis climbed eagerly up in his high
> chair, apparently ready to do another thorough job of

eating his dinner. However, this time he had another idea, and he couldn't wait to try it. He sat back in his chair, crossed his arms and announced, 'I won't eat.' . . . I did some quick thinking. It scared me that he might not eat, because I had seen how crabby he could be when he got hungry. I also realized that he could get me to do lots of things, some of them rather awful, like begging, or threatening, or playing games (here comes the choo-choo), or bribing to get him to eat. All of it would make me look very silly and he still wouldn't eat. So I said, 'That's all right, you don't have to eat. Just sit here and keep us company while we eat.' He looked absolutely crestfallen. It seemed like such a good game, and I just wouldn't play.[5]

Creative parenting requires a quick wit and a good sense of humour.

CHAPTER THREE

The Heartland of Childhood

The Grade School Years

The thing that impresses me most about America is the way parents obey their children.

— EDWARD, DUKE OF WINDSOR

Crossing the Mississippi, we enter America's Heartland. This land engenders a new feeling, especially for those like me who were raised on the east coast. There is an expansive quality to the Midwest landscape that alters our sense of time and space. Distances are greater, vistas endless, and hurrying seems pointless. Speech slows, movements slow, and everyday activities like drinking a cup of coffee take longer. The land just west of the Mississippi is predictable, and in some places, like Iowa, it is just plain heavenly.

Children have their heartland as well and it usually starts around the age of seven. When they cross the Mississippi, children begin to live even more strongly in their feelings and a new emphasis is established. An awareness of this change needs to be incorporated into our parenting.

Our children begin to show evidence of a changing inner landscape. These inner alterations can be found in many places, even in children's games. While these games may seem like just 'child's play,' they actually teach children very important lessons for this stage of development. Games like 'Mother, May I?' and 'Red Light, Green Light' enable six and seven year olds to begin to consciously regulate and control their own impulsivity. Playing games like these helps them find their way into this region of childhood where a new awareness is dawning. Older brothers and sisters also teach their younger siblings these important lessons. Young children instinctively know if they want to play with the older children, they must follow the rules. They understand that they can't just do what they feel like doing.

One popular and revealing game for children at this age is Simon Says. To be successful at Simon Says, children must be able to resist the impulse to imitate. In doing this, they are being asked to exercise control over what was previously, in the early childhood years, an uncontrollable urge. In this game, it is not acceptable just to do what others do. A child whose urge to imitate is immediate and unrestrained and who simply mimics the movement of hands to the head or hands to the knees, is out. But if the authorized command of Simon Says is spoken, then the movement is sanctioned and the game continues.

Recently, I was in downtown Washington, D.C. on a weekend afternoon when I came upon a cluster of inner-city boys, some teenagers, some younger, all dressed in baggy pants and hooded sweatshirts. They were all rollerblading on the sidewalk. Each one got a turn to skate quickly down the sidewalk, and then suddenly leap up about fifteen inches, do a 360 degree spin and land on the long, flat ledge of a rectangular stone planter. At this point, they continued skating another ten feet before leaping back down. They did this in perfect order, one after another, at even intervals of about twenty seconds. No one argued, no one pushed, no one went out of turn. The older boys had simply worked out this arrangement on their own and the younger ones followed suit.

In years past, neighbourhoods, schoolyards, sidewalks, playgrounds all provided informal opportunities for children to play in unstructured and unsupervised multi-age settings, situations that enabled them to teach

each other important lessons. Today, there is less of this as we tend to plan and regulate our children's playtime. However, even without the benefit of informal, child-led opportunities such as these, we can expect children to acquire the ability to suppress what they feel like doing and do what they need to or are expected to do.

If we look at the words of Daniel Goleman, author of the best-selling book, *Emotional Intelligence*, we see that this learning has implications for who our children will be as adults.

> There is growing evidence that fundamental ethical stances in life stem from underlying emotional capacities; the seed of all impulses is feeling bursting to express itself in action. Those who are at the mercy of impulse — who lack self-control suffer moral deficiency. The ability to control impulse is the basis of will and character.[6]

Another place where children used to be able to learn this lesson, so fundamental to self-discipline, was in school. Today, however, that appears to have changed. In a large city school where I worked recently, it was common for some students to come to class ten minutes late. When one English teacher asked a tardy student to give her a note explaining his lateness, the student wrote: 'I was late because I forgot what time it was. If you don't like it, so what.' Teachers, across the country, can attest that this sort of response is not unique and that our standards for acceptable behaviour are declining. Amidst such declining standards, many schools don't even bother to check homework assignments or respond to foul language.

Without schools or playgrounds to help teach these lessons, parents are left to do this important work on their own. Children now depend almost entirely on parents to teach them how to discriminate between what they feel like doing and what they shouldn't do. During the second phase of childhood, starting from around the age of six or seven, this is a parent's essential undertaking.

A Paradoxical Dilemma

> One of the remarkable aspects of being human (is) to
> hold opposing views in one's mind at once.

> — TERRY TEMPEST WILLIAMS, *An Unspoken Hunger*

Having stated that young people need to learn to separate what they feel like doing from what they actually do, I hear a voice within me rising up in disagreement. It reminds me that there are times when the opposite statement is also true, when we should marry our feelings to our actions, do what we love and pursue our passionate interests. In fact, those instances may be the most important undertakings of our lives.

The distinction I want to make is this: If, during the course of childhood, children haven't been helped to develop the capacity to finish their homework or the job they're doing even when friends are outside playing, they may not be able to distinguish between those special moments when they need to follow their heart and those other times when they need to just say 'No.' This is a complex understanding that only develops over time. It requires a higher form of intelligence, one that depends on the maturation of our brains. But it is also highly dependent on the willingness of mothers and fathers to assume the role of parental authorities and to help children learn these lessons at an early age.

Avoiding Authority

A young couple arrives at a restaurant with their two children for dinner. They take off their coats, sit at a table for four, and begin to go over the menu. Judging from the familiarity of the conversation around ordering, this is an event that has taken place before. After the order is placed, the older son, who is around seven, gets up to wander around the restaurant and is soon followed by his younger sister who looks to be about five years old. Before long, these two children are running around the restaurant, between the tables, climbing in and out of the empty booths playing tag.

As the parents wait for the food to arrive, the play becomes more animated and disturbing to the other patrons. Looks are exchanged and the mother gets up once or twice to speak to the children. But their vigorous play is only quietened temporarily. The mother is obviously embarrassed and calls quietly for them to stop, but the father seems oblivious to the ruckus his children are creating. Finally, to the relief of many, the food arrives and the children rush to their table. Just before the older boy is seated the father pulls him to his lap and it appears that he is finally going to say something to the boy about his behaviour. Instead, with an expression of pure delight and unaffected love, he hugs and kisses his child.

I found this scene both disturbing and reassuring, but by no means unique. I have seen similar situations acted out in concerts, school events, and in stores when parents avoid the role of the authority and choose instead to be the purveyors of love.

There is an important lesson here, a riddle to be solved, and it has to do with the mysterious nature of paradox and the important role it plays in human life. Many of today's parents, and particularly fathers, grew up experiencing authority in the form of unrelenting and unfeeling structure. Consequently, they have shunned this notion of authority in favour of a warm, nurturing and embracing relationship with their children. They have rejected the past emphasis on parental firmness and have opted instead to accentuate understanding and affection. So when their children feel like running around a restaurant, they remember how hard it was to sit quietly for the long period of time that it takes for a meal to be prepared and they choose to ignore their children's behaviour. But in choosing to travel this route, parents encourage behaviour (and, of course, misbehaviour) that is inconsiderate of others and which will eventually disappoint them, as well.

I was in a fathering workshop last spring in Napa, California, and was interested to hear what challenges these fathers faced. As we went around the circle, these young dads expressed again and again how their children's behaviour was a concern to them and how they longed for the right way to get their children to behave properly. They lamented that too often, when their patience was finally exhausted, which happens eventually to even the most nurturing parents, they ended up responding in ways that they abhorred and said and did things they swore they would never say or do to their children. To avoid this unpleasant and all too common experience, many fathers choose by default to sidestep the role of being an authority.

This is the challenge and the opportunity that many parents face today. To bring wholeness to our parenting we must come to see that we need to embrace both aspects of this paradox — firmness and loving understanding — and weave them together so that we become loving authorities. Parker Palmer expressed this best in his excellent book, *The Courage to Teach*, when he stated, "Neils Bohr, the Nobel prize winning physicist, offers the keystone I want to build on: 'The opposite of a true statement is a false statement, but the opposite of a profound truth can also be another profound truth.'" [7]

It is true that children need understanding. The opposite is also true: children need firmness. When parents recognize that children need both understanding and firmness and that these can be provided in an emotional climate that is both protective and strengthening, discipline becomes a positive experience for all. To achieve this, we must redefine authority and expand its definition to include the kind of emotional responses that we feel are essential to a healthy parent-child relationship.

Authority, Authenticity, and Authorship

The word authority has the same root as the words author and authentic. They all derive from the Latin word *auctoritas*, which translates to author, authority, or originator.

When the word authority is connected to authorship and authenticity, it begins to lose its stigma and can be seen as a creative, original, position of influence through which parents try to convey their deeply held, heartfelt values to their children.

If discipline is to be authentic, then it must be about those values that are near and dear to us — not necessarily our neighbours', our parents', nor our culture's values. To find these values which are at the heart of authentic discipline, parents need to do some soul-searching, both at the beginning of the parenting journey and along the way, especially at those moments when we feel the aching disappointment that tells us something in our parenting is not right. If we take the time to explore these feelings, we will discover our aspirations and longings as parents. These longings are integral to authentic parenting and at the core of what will make us authorities in the truest sense.

Good parenting is not about an elaborate, delineated system of beliefs; rather, it is about simple understandings. These can be as simple as how we speak to each other, how we share the work that needs to be done in the home, and how we meet and interact at the dinner table. Once these core values emerge, (and that is really what they are) then we begin to author the script (call it a family mission statement) that allows these values to become real in our home. Because these values are unique to us, our script is original; we are the authors. We don't embrace these values to impress others or to oppress our children, but rather to quietly convey to those dearest to us what we believe is important and what we hope, one day, they will value as well.

The busyness of modern life often keeps us from paying attention to what is most important. We move from the school-run to work, from shopping to children's football. We don't have time to reflect. But sometimes events intervene — an illness, the death of a loved one, or a catastrophe like September 11th — and make us stop and take stock of what truly matters.

Tragic events teach us most emphatically that life is too short to ignore what matters most — our family. It is out of this commitment that we take up our parental responsibility of being an authority for the sake of our children. Then, with keen and sensitive observation, regular introspection, and repeated conversations with our spouse or other involved adults, we create a home that reflects what we value, with the understanding that in the long run these values will support and gladden the hearts of everyone in our family.

Besides, we must always keep in mind that children want boundaries. Boundaries give them a security that allows them to push the limits yet still be held safe. It is why kids invariably love firm teachers and demanding coaches if they are fair and caring and enjoy what they do. Discipline is a parent's responsibility. So much depends on how we respond emotionally to this challenge. Authority and discipline must always be concerned with feelings, the feelings that live in the children and the feelings that live in us, the parents, when we discipline.

Effective parenting continually evolves. In the first phase of childhood, from birth to around the age of seven, what matters most is what we do. Our actions and our willingness to be actively involved with our children are of the greatest significance. More will be asked of us in the second stage of childhood. West of the Mississippi another aspect of parenting will need greater emphasis. What we do with a child of seven, eight, or nine still matters, but what we feel — that is, what we convey emotionally — matters most of all.

Parents' Feelings Teach

Our feelings and the way in which we express those feelings will instruct our children. All the admirable emotional qualities that we want our children to develop, qualities like empathy, resilience, joyfulness, and gratitude are best taught by example. This is pointed out by T. Berry Brazelton and Stanley Greenspan in their book, *The Irreducible Needs of Children*.

> They [children] learn . . . not just from what we say but from how we relate to them and how we say it. Therefore, empathy, for example, is taught not by telling children to be nice to others or to try to understand others, but by parents' having the patience to listen to children and children's feeling understood. Once they understand what empathy feels like, they

can create it in their relationships. Similarly, love can be described at length, but unless we've felt love, we may not have an emotional reference point to understand what it means. We have to experience these complicated feelings ourselves to understand them and to learn how to use them with others.[8]

Our emotional life matters to our children because they are keenly sensitive to what we feel. They will detect our feelings in our facial expressions, in our tone of voice, even in our posture. That is why we can be standing in the kitchen doing the same thing that we have done a hundred times before and our children, detecting a different mood, will ask, 'Is something wrong, Mummy?'

Feelings colour a child's perceptions. When I was in fifth grade, already eleven years old, I had a long-term substitute teacher whom I really liked. I remember saying to my mum that I thought my teacher was beautiful. She didn't agree at all and told me that my teacher was really quite plain, but I never saw her that way. To me, she was always sweet and kind and that made her lovely, much lovelier than the 'attractive' teacher she had replaced who was impatient, a little snappy, and easily annoyed.

This middle stage, the primary school years, is the Heartland of Childhood. During this time children will experience the world strongly through feelings. This presents a challenge to all parents, and particularly to fathers.

In years past, emotional responsiveness was not part of a father's job description. One look at the male role models in post-World War II America reveals emotionally inaccessible men. John Wayne and Charlton Heston were men of action and savvy, but not feelings. Even Humphrey Bogart, whose emotions seemed to roil beneath the surface in Casablanca, never managed to express the sadness and disappointment that he felt.

These figures, along with early sitcom dads, reflected the times in which they lived. A half century ago, it was acceptable for fathers to conduct their lives with emotional distance. Many of today's fathers were raised by men who did just that. If a father had a disappointing or upsetting time at work, the children were told, 'Leave your father alone. He's had a hard day.'

If we look at how fathers have been portrayed more recently, we can see a change from previous norms. Tom Hanks gave an inspiring performance as a great dad in *Sleepless in Seattle*. His late night radio conversation conveyed beautifully his love for his deceased wife and for his son.

Another extraordinary portrayal of an emotionally responsive father was given by Roberto Benigni in *Life Is Beautiful*. His character had that remarkable light heartedness that can brighten any home. In addition, he was able to remain inwardly joyful and playful in the midst of the most horrendous circumstances. Through his vibrant emotional life he was able to protect his son.

This sense that life is beautiful is an essential characteristic of good parenting. It will create a climate in which discipline will be more readily accepted and more easily borne.

Back to Bedtime

Now if we return to the bedtime discussion from the previous chapter, we will be able to see how discipline can be more palatable paired with the right feelings. To begin with it must be noted that the very best discipline is preventive discipline. If we have begun the parenting journey on the right foot, we will have already spent a couple of years east of the Mississippi establishing good bedtime habits by modelling a positive example and by establishing a consistent routine. Still, somewhere around the age of seven or eight we will need to add a little something to the routine to freshen it up. What we want most of all is for bedtime to be special so that we can avoid whining, crying, and procrastination. Our remedy is to create the right emotional climate around the routines of bath and bedtime because these will influence our children's attitudes. If our mood is light-hearted and undistracted, we will succeed.

To do this, we must build special touches into the structure of bath and bedtime. For instance, we can make bath-time alluring by making the bathroom environment beautiful with gentle lighting, folded towels, and a soft bathrobe. These measures work for adults and they also work for children. Touches that make a difference can be as simple as having a special soap, fragrant bath oil, bubble bath, or a favourite wash cloth. It is similar with bedtime. Children are often eager to get into a newly made bed with clean sheets and a fresh pillowcase.

When my daughter was six or seven, I was on a business trip to Atlanta and was in Hartsfield Airport with about fifteen minutes to spare before my plane began boarding. I decided to see if I could find a little gift to bring her. I am not the best shopper and so I knew that I needed a little luck. I went into *The Body Shop* looking for one of those cute little nail cleaning brushes shaped like a duck or a whale. Then I saw the perfect gift. It was a puppet, a pink elephant, and a washcloth all in one. It was both inexpensive and priceless — it delighted my daughter for months. Although this pink elephant has since been retired from active duty, it still resides in my fifteen-year-old daughter's room on her bookcase.

There are other desirable bath-time comforts, including warm towels or pyjamas. Few children can resist their towel, nightgown or pyjamas warmed in the dryer or by the woodstove in winter. Knowing that these simple pleasures await them at the end of the bath is the perfect motivation for them to begin.

One other possible lure (not bribe) is to end bath-time with a cup of something warm and soothing to drink. Many children enjoy an opportunity to sit on the couch after a warm bath and sip a hot drink. This provides a time to transition to bedtime as well as a chance for some reflective conversation at the end of a long day. When there is time to add these special moments to the routine, they can provide the leaven that keeps the daily routine from sinking into the heaviness of tedium.

I want to digress a moment to distinguish between bribes and lures. I don't believe in bribing children. A bribe assumes that a child is not going to do what you're asking. That is an assumption that I try not to make because it undermines my effectiveness as a parent. A lure or an incentive, on the other hand, entices the child to head in the right direction in a timely manner.

The Great Expansive Plains

The basic premise of *Navigating the Terrain of Childhood* is that the geography of our continent has something to teach us about our children. That is certainly true when we look at the expansiveness of the Great Plains.

Middle childhood, at its very best, has its wide-open spaces, cloudless stretches of blue sky and vast areas of open land. Picture a boy, like my younger son, who regularly began his Saturdays in front of the house with a football and a goal or a hockey stick, a net, and a puck. He played by himself for an hour or two before anyone was ready to be as active as he was. Then, at the end of the day, after the rest of us had been tired out by his boundless energy, he returned to the street to practise some more — dozens of field goals, hundreds of slap shots — just bookends on the great expanse of Saturday.

These wonderful stretches of free time allow children to relax, to breathe out, and to encounter the creative opportunities that reside on the other side of boredom. Unfortunately, our children today have decreasing amounts of unscheduled time. Non-school time is divided up into soccer practice, football games, karate lessons, ballet, gymnastics, horse riding, and more. Many children are fully booked and because of this stress levels rise.

To complicate matters further, parents of busy children are also overextended. Far too often, we find ourselves rushing through traffic, either with, or in pursuit of, our children, trying desperately to be on time. As we hurry our shoulders tighten, our hands tense around the steering wheel, and our voices take on an edge. We become hurried parents heading toward a head-on collision with our hurried children — all of us strung tighter than we need to be.

This is a significant change that has occurred over the last fifty years. When I look at my parents' lives, I am struck by dramatic differences. My mother walked to her part-time job at our neighbourhood primary school, never drove on the school-run, and never returned home to a series of e-mail or phone messages. Neither she nor my father travelled as part of their jobs or worked evenings and weekends. Although my wife and I would not want to give up the social changes that have taken place in recent decades, we can't help but notice how different our lifestyle is from our parents' and we can't help but be a little envious. They simply had less complicated lives.

Our schedules are so tenuous that any little glitch can wreak havoc. A maths assignment from hell, a library book forgotten at school, an unexpected traffic delay, an automobile problem — any one of these can expose our shortcomings and move us and our children toward a crisis.

Compressed time significantly impacts our ability to relate to our children. Whenever I speak with parents of primary-school children about the problems that occur in the home, I am repeatedly reminded that our difficult parenting moments are fairly predictable. These moments often occur before dinner or at bedtime, especially when dinner is a little late. Or they happen in the morning, when everyone is getting ready for the school bus or the school-run. These times can be particularly trying if dinner and bedtime the night before were late. All of these instances are important transition times and all are more difficult to manage when time, sleep and energy (food) is in short supply.

When time constraints cause parents to rush their children, difficulties are more likely to arise. Because children at this age are so sensitive to feelings, our tensions become their tensions. When tension increases, our children's character traits become more exaggerated. Sensitive children become whiny and weepy; fiery energetic children throw fits; placid children become stubborn and resistant; and light-hearted, carefree children become distracted and forgetful. Thankfully, just an extra ten minutes at these transition times can make all the difference. Having enough time allows us all to exhale and breathe deeply, to relax, and to smile. If we can add extra time to each challenging transition, our parenting will improve.

A slow Midwestern lifestyle is just what we need in our families in this middle phase of childhood, especially when it comes to dinner. This is one of the most challenging times for hurried families. Low blood sugar and general fatigue often leave children (and parents) vulnerable, and when the time before dinner is tense and volatile, it is hard for the mealtime to be pleasant. Dinner is a central event for families because it sets the tone for our family life, but it is by no means easy. Parent educator Inda Schaenen urges parents to start dinner early. An early dinner 'makes conversation possible. Young children are not so strung out that they ruin the meal for everyone. (And) older children are usually happy to talk at this (earlier) hour.'[9] With a head start and a little breathing room, mealtimes can become a place where the bond between parents and children is strengthened rather than tested.

The Basis of True Authority

Family time plays a significant role in our parenting during this second phase of childhood. It provides us with the opportunity to strengthen the emotional bond that we have with our children. The emotional bond that forms between parent and child through shared activities, celebrations, and experiences will warm and soften all of the discipline that is needed at this stage.

This is key because parental authority is not a position that we just assume. It is one that is given to us by our children and we must earn it. When our children are young, they grant us authority out of their childlike love and devotion. But as they grow older — nine, ten, and beyond — our authority will depend more on how we respond to disciplinary situations. If we are calm, consistent, and caring, our children will continue to accept our guidance. If we are rushed, tense, and short-tempered, resistance will surface. As children grow, their acceptance of authority is more selective. This acceptance of authority will last if it is based on love and respect, not on fear of punishment.

True authority depends on a wide variety of factors. It depends on parents maintaining a positive attitude, one that is able to continually separate bad behaviour from a child's innate goodness. True authority also depends on a reflex of self-discipline, on our ability to recognise enthusiastic interpretations of our own foibles in our children's worst traits, and on our willingness to work to overcome these traits in ourselves. But above all, true authority is a loving authority and as such it rests on a warm and caring foundation.

Even with the best intentions, disciplinary situations will create distance between children and parents. Even if we view discipline as a guiding, creative principle and establish it early and painlessly through good habits and routines, a time will come when our discipline will need to wear a sterner face. Similarly, even though we view authority as authentic, original, and loving guidance, there will still come a time when we will need to be consequent and unyielding. It is unavoidable. As our children grow, they need to test boundaries and limits. And this limit-testing is what we must expect when we prepare to cross the Missouri River.

CHAPTER FOUR

Crossing the Missouri River

Turning Ten and Beyond

> When a child first catches adults out — when it first walks into his grave little head that adults do not have divine intelligence, that their judgments are not always wise, their thinking true, their sentences just — his world falls into panic desolation. The gods are fallen and all safety gone. And there is one sure thing about the fall of the gods; they do not fall a little; they crash . . . And the child's world is never quite whole again. It is an aching kind of growing.
>
> — JOHN STEINBECK, *East of Eden*

I t is 4pm and quiet has finally descended on the main office of a local public school. The halls are still, the children have gone home or to aftercare, and the teachers are closing their classroom doors and departing. Only the principal remains. Now that the others have gone, she can settle down and focus on the meeting that she has scheduled with a social worker and an educator from an organization that has been funded to provide support services for 'at risk' children.

This principal exemplifies good leadership. She courteously dispenses with formalities and focuses on the services her children need. 'Yes,' she says, 'I can use some help for my teachers in classes one, two, and three. But what I really need is help for the teachers of my older children because something changes in my students between the third and fourth classes. After that, their problems can become much more severe.'

The principal is alluding to a change that can be best described as an awakening. This awakening occurs strongly around the age of nine or ten when children begin to see the world in more detail. This increased dose of reality leaves some children fearful, others dispirited, and in some situations, it leaves them angry. Although this change is not often written up in child development texts, it has been poignantly captured in the following lines from the poet Billy Collins:

On Turning Ten

But now I am mostly at the window
watching the late afternoon light.
Back then it never fell so solemnly
against the side of my tree house,
and my bicycle never leaned against the garage
as it does today,
all the dark blue speed drained out of it.

This is the beginning of sadness, I say to myself,
as I walk through the universe in my sneakers.
It is time to say good-bye to my imaginary friends,
time to turn the first big number.

It seems only yesterday I used to believe
there was nothing under my skin but light.
If you cut me I would shine.
But now when I fall upon the sidewalks of life,
I skin my knees. I bleed.[10]

This is an inward change, one that transpires quietly, privately, and sometimes solemnly in the lives of children. Not every child experiences this change at exactly the same time. For some this loss of innocence happens before nine, especially when life's disappointments, like divorce or death, impact at an early age. With other children, it can occur a year or two later. But regardless of the timing, the signs are the same. Children become self-conscious, distant, more belligerent, and more alone in the world. There are fewer kisses in public and more closed doors in private. There can be muttering and back talk. We are entering the Badlands of Childhood and it is often hard for parents to see that these changes in their child's behaviour are a necessary part of their development. In fact, they are.

Every parent hopes that the journey through childhood is a journey toward independence. Our children start out needing us for everything, but if we do our job well, we make ourselves redundant in the end. Independence develops gradually over time, but there are certain places in the journey through childhood where the shift toward independence is more noticeable. Somewhere west of the age of nine such a shift occurs. It is like crossing the Missouri River. Once we are on the other side, the land begins to change dramatically.

These developmental junctures, when a child's sense of self increases markedly, present challenges for parents. Each thrust of self-awareness comes with a corresponding amount of independence and accompanying new behaviours. Although these behaviours often look and feel just like unruliness, there is more going on. At these times, our children are taking on some of the responsibility of ruling themselves — certainly a work in progress. A child's growing sense of self makes their own wants and wishes sound more loudly than before, often obscuring what we expect of them or what we have asked them to do. Some parents respond to this change by turning up the volume of their requests;

others respond by repeating themselves again and again; and a few just throw up their hands out of frustration. But if we want to respond appropriately to the inevitable challenges that await us at this stage, we must remind ourselves that this is exactly what is supposed to happen.

Once we cross the Missouri River, we leave behind the predictable and uneventful Plains. The terrain immediately becomes more striking, but also more challenging. It is exactly the same with children. During the first nine or ten years, events are easier to predict. There is a comforting consistency and continuity to the first half of childhood. The routines and habits that we establish in the early years make us feel that life is orderly and secure and as parents we are doing a good job. But around the age of nine or ten, these assessments are called into question.

I remember the first sign that our daughter was entering this new region. For several years, she had been very good about getting herself ready for bed and so I was well aware that she knew exactly what to do. My job was easy. I had simply to watch and listen and oversee from a distance.

One evening she was reading a book when her mother asked her to get ready for bed. I watched her close the book, walk down the hallway, and turn into the bathroom. I saw the light go on and heard the water begin to run; all seemed to be in order. But several minutes later the water was still running, and so I decided to take a look. When I passed the bathroom door, which fortunately was open, there was my daughter standing in the bathroom reading while the water ran down the drain.

This was a new behaviour for her, but because she was the third child, I had seen this kind of variation before and that helped give me some perspective. I did not lose my patience and lecture her about the amount of water being wasted, the depth of the water table, the height of the water bill, or about trust and responsibility (I'd save that last conversation for when it was really needed). I simply said, 'Oh my, you've forgotten how to get ready for bed. I'll have to help you.' Her reply was instantaneous, 'Oh no, I remember!' and she immediately put the book down and started to wash.

It is important to keep in mind that these kinds of transgressions are part of normal child development at this age. They are not a measure of parental ineffectiveness or of some character flaw in our child. A parent's task is simply to remain calm and always to be rational. Calm, rational responses are just what children want and expect at this age.

The Badlands of Anger

> Anyone can become angry — that is easy. But to be angry with the right person, to the right degree, at the right time, for the right purpose, and in the right way — this is not easy.
>
> — ARISTOTLE, *The Nicomachean Ethics*

I am not a perfect father, but I am a much better father when I am not surprised. When my children's behaviour catches me off guard, I can get angry and over-react. In his excellent booklet *Reflections on Discipline*, John Gardner wrote:

> Is it too much to say that most parents associate the disciplinary situation with anger? A child does what he should not do or fails to do what he should, and we become angry. Things do not go as we want: anger flares. Why is this?
>
> Of course, some of us are more prone to anger than others. There are violent natures and placid natures. But when it comes to dealing with their own children, even the placid often find themselves at the edge . . . Generally speaking, we become angry when we are too weak to cope with a situation. Anger is our attempt to redouble our strength. If a little anger carries us through the obstacle we cool readily; but if not, we may develop a towering rage.[11]

Around the age of nine or ten, our children may do things that are much more perplexing than letting the water run down the drain. Sometimes these behaviours will inconvenience us, such as when a child runs off to play and can't be found when it's the school-run's pick-up time. At other times, the behaviours will cause us concern as when our child forgets to mention that she has homework until just before bedtime. And sometimes the behaviours will frighten us (often this is when parents get the angriest), such as when a child decides to go off to play at a friend's house without letting us know.

Most children are creative and have a special talent for picking the most challenging times to experiment with new (mis)behaviours. The hardest task for a parent is to encounter these situations calmly especially when they occur at stress-filled moments. At those times, it is difficult not to take the timing of the misbehaviour personally and mutter through clenched teeth: 'Why is this happening to me today of all days? I'm stressed. I've had a hard day. Why now?'

Yet, I believe that if we had statistics on children's misbehaviours, even those that seem so personal, we would find that they happen in a similar way in many families. When I speak to parents, I often ask, 'How many of you have stubborn, strong-minded children?' Invariably, three-quarters of the parents raise their hands. That is why we should mark this region on the map of childhood and make a note to remind ourselves that somewhere on the other side of the Missouri River these kinds of unexpected events can be expected. Then, when they occur, we can refer to the map and say to ourselves: 'This is normal. How do I want to respond?' I would suggest calmly, with a knowing smile, and above all, with consequences.

Consequences

A number of years ago, I was teaching a group of nine and ten year olds. At the time, our school had a rule that children were not allowed to eat out in the playground. This rule had been put into effect several years before because plastic bags and juice boxes were often left littering the asphalt at the end of lunchtime. In the early classes, the students were very good about abiding by this school rule, but the third and fourth years usually tested the limits.

One day in my third-year class, I noticed that a sweet, active boy had put his lunch away very quickly and was ready to go out to play. As he walked to the back of the classroom, I could see that he had his hand placed conspicuously in his pocket. The gesture reminded me of all the times that I tried to conceal objects from my parents or my teachers. So I stood up calmly as he left and followed him to the playground where I encountered him eating his cookie. I greeted him, smiled, noted his cookie, and the fact that he was eating outside. Then I calmly asked him to come back to the classroom. We returned to the room and he sat down at his desk while the other children put their things away and went outside. I sat at my desk, said nothing, and did some paperwork. He sat meekly finishing his cookie with little bites and then after a couple of minutes asked, 'Can I go out now?'

'No,' I replied, calmly without looking up. I let him sit there in silence for a few more minutes knowing that now was the time when he really wished he had not eaten on the playground and when the lesson was being learned. When I did speak with him about five minutes later, I reminded him of the school rules but I also told him that I always enjoyed his company and was glad to spend my lunchtime with him. So if he took food outside, I would be happy to sit with him again, perhaps for a couple of lunches. There was no rancour and I was not upset. He was a good boy, just doing his job of testing the limits, and I was just doing my job as an adult upholding them.

This may seem like a big deal to make over a cookie. But it was a conscious and deliberate transgression on his part, which shouldn't be ignored. This is a lesson that we need to convey to our children early on. If we miss the opportunity to be consequent with our children at this early stage when they first ignore the rules, they will certainly give us other chances, but often the stakes will be higher. When teenagers ignore their curfew or drive faster than the speed limit, or sneak out at night after their parents are asleep, the potential hazards are far greater. A parent's response to the smaller transgressions sets the tone for the later years.

It is so important that we send this serious message calmly. When we lose our temper, it causes upset both in us and in our children and can make us say things we later regret. This leaves us feeling that we have failed, and this disappointment obscures the fact that we did not cause this problem; our children's behaviour did. It is far more effective if we temper our anger at the moment of the transgression and transform it into a quiet resolve to be rational.

When our sons were nine and thirteen, they developed the habit of responding to all requests with the one word response, 'Fine.' What made this situation problematic was that this ostensibly positive term was always delivered with an emphatic, negative intonation.

'Would you please start your homework?'

'Fine!'

'Would you please do the dishes?'

'Fine!'

After a few weeks of these unpleasant interactions my wife and I realized that something needed to be done. We talked it over and I set to work with my calligraphy pen and made up little cards that simply said, 'No Dessert.' I coloured the cards in nicely with a different colour for each child. Then my wife and I sat down to speak with our sons. We proceeded to tell them that they were great kids and mentioned a number of their positive traits. We also expressed our worry that they were developing a bad habit of responding to requests rudely. We told them that we wanted to help them with this and that each time they spoke rudely we would simply post (without further warning) one of the 'No Dessert' cards on the refrigerator and the next time we had dessert there would be none for the individual with the posted card.

Well, it wasn't long before we got an opportunity to use the cards. Rude words passed, the card was posted, and after dinner that night when the ice cream was served, there were three bowls of ice cream instead of four. I can still see my son's jaw drop in disbelief as he realized that there was dessert at every place except his. There was a look of recognition as if to say, 'You meant it?' But there was also a marked change in his behaviour from that moment on.

Consequences are more about actions than lectures. As a rule, most parents today talk too much in disciplinary situations. Too much talking just opens the door for an argument, and children are incredible lawyers. The further west we go, children will find more and more opportunities to say, 'I think you're making too big a deal out of this . . .' 'All my friends do this . . .' 'Nobody else's parents,' etc. It may be that some of these conversations are needed and that the conversation may also need to be a dialogue. But it is absolutely appropriate for parents to have the last word. 'Well, you know, I am not everyone else's parent. I'm your parent and I care about you. What you did was not right and that is why the following is going to occur . . .'

Sometimes we may have to delay this conversation until everyone has calmed down. It is certainly acceptable for a parent to say, 'I can't speak to you about this right now, but I will talk with you later. Please go to your room. There will be consequences.' This keeps us from making rash statements on the spot that we will later regret and helps us avoid saying things that we have to take back.

Having stated all this, I want to say something on behalf of all of those children who test the limits of our patience. Strong children often misbehave in strong ways and call on us to find strengths we are not sure we have. These misbehaviours are not symptomatic of a character flaw; rather, they are an indication of a strong disposition to live life to the fullest. Though it might not always seem so, this is good news. If our children are going to make a difference in tomorrow's world and grow up to be sturdy individuals, they will have to be determinedly stubborn to stand up to peer pressure, special interests, bureaucracy, and a world full of seemingly insolvable problems. These challenging children are the hope of the future, but we must help them see that there are limits by which they must abide. Unwavering parental authority helps strong children find their way on their road to self-discipline.

At first glance, this may seem a counter-intuitive understanding of what children need. It is easy to think that if we want our children to acquire self-discipline, make decisions for themselves, and regulate their own behaviour, we should hand the reins over at an early age. But children don't come fully equipped to direct their own lives. In fact, many of the most challenging individuals often do not demonstrate the ability to fully take charge of their lives until they are in their early twenties. But we can be optimistic. With consistent and determined parenting, intractable children do grow up to be responsible adults.

The road to self-discipline runs through all the regions of the country. It starts out on the east coast in small ways with children learning to clean up their toys and to tie their own shoes. It shifts to sharing in family work in the middle phase, when children clear the table, clean the dishes, and begin to clean their own room. And once past the Missouri River, it happens as our children take responsibility for getting themselves to a friend's house either by walking or riding a bike. Beyond the Rockies, it evolves even further with babysitting, gardening, and eventually part-time jobs, situations where the expectations for behaviour are set by others, not just by us. Parenting is a long-term project, one that gradually moves our children from dependence to independence.

Timing is Everything

When is the right time for a parent to relinquish authority? During teacher training, I learned a lesson that helped me to understand the answer to this question. In a child development class, I was asked to imagine an archer who wanted to send an arrow into the distance. The professor noted that conventional logic would make you think that the first thing the archer should do if he wants to shoot an arrow is to push the bowstring forward. However, we all know that it is far more effective to pull the bowstring back in the 'wrong' direction. In fact, the farther the archer wants the arrow to go, the more strongly he pulls the bowstring the other way. Like an accomplished bowman, parents are asked to draw their children toward them through imitation and authority. Then, in the face of increasing tension and resistance, a parent must hold steady and continue to pull the arrow back a little more until the time is just right for letting go. In this way, they will send their children furthest on the journey toward independence.

As our children move toward adolescence, with the continental divide of the teenage years looming on the horizon, we will feel that tension increase, but it is certainly not time to let go.

The Black Hills and the Big Horn Mountains — Easing into Adolescence

As our children move toward adolescence, with the continental divide of the teenage years looming on the horizon, we will feel the tension increase, but it is certainly not time to let go. The fact is that once we cross the Missouri River, the parenting journey hits a rougher road with an increasing number of uphill climbs and precipitous descents. Heading into the foothills of the Rockies (around the age of twelve) we begin to have parenting experiences that we have not seen previously and they are a harbinger of what lies ahead. Descending through a Big Horn Mountain pass in June, it is common to find the streams full with spring melt. They rush with a force and a colour that you rarely see back east. There is urgency in these raging streams, a power that reminds us of the adolescent. Like the surging hormonal changes brought on by puberty, these streams display a force that cannot be turned back.

Something strong and new is dawning in our children with the onset of puberty which now comes earlier than ever before. For the girls, noticeable physical changes begin even before the age of twelve. They mirror strong psychological changes that are occurring as well. Along with dramatic fluctuations in a young person's emotional life, there are signs of changes in thinking. Critical thinking is emerging in the young person and this often takes the form of growing criticism of parents and teachers. It can help to think of adolescence in its beginning stages as a pregnancy, a time in which something new is about to be born. This helped me to understand some of the facial expressions my daughter made at this age in response to my everyday questions or remarks. When she rolled her eyes or grimaced at what she perceived as a ridiculous question or an unbelievably embarrassing comment, I would tell myself that this was like morning sickness, a temporary phase that would eventually pass.

Boys also experience this pregnancy and in some instances it may manifest in a similar way. But it also shows itself in a boy's tendency to withdraw from the family and to isolate himself in his room with his radio, books, or video games.

Like a pregnancy, the onset of adolescence also affects memory. Brain research shows that the adolescent brain is being both deconstructed and restructured at this time. So if it seems as though twelve- and thirteen-year-old boys find it hard to remember the simplest things that we worked so hard to teach them, there is scientific evidence to show why this occurs.

So much is going on in the life of adolescents. From a physical perspective, their bodies are going through massive hormonal, skeletal, muscular, and neurological changes. Psychologically and socially they are confronting unpredictability and uncertainty. With this next thrust of increased self-awareness around twelve, similar in many ways to what happened around the age of nine, comes a dramatic increase in the powers of observation. Our children now begin to recognise and generalize about behaviour patterns and shortcomings in others. This is one of the ways they develop the capacity for critical thinking, an important tool that children will need for independence. But as they begin to use this increasingly sharp and probing faculty in the early stages of adolescence, it can be hazardous to others. To help our children learn to use this new faculty positively, we must continue to provide them with guidance as well as a balancing structure of consistent activities and a climate of emotional respect and protection.

This past weekend, I worked with a group of parents in North Carolina who wanted to know how they could raise their children in a manner that resulted in healthy independence. Even though they lived in an uncertain and seemingly unsafe world, they did not want to raise timid children. They struggled to know the right time to allow their children to take the next big steps.

West of the Missouri River, our children will want to test themselves and live more dangerously. We should help them find safe venues for this experience, understanding that they will seek them anyway. In her insightful book, *The Blessing of a Skinned Knee: Using Jewish Teachings to Raise Self-Reliant Children*, Wendy Mogel speaks about the need to allow children to take reasonable risks. She notes that if we don't allow our children to take chances, we will raise them to be timid, unwilling to push through the 'narrow places' or 'blockages.' Mogel uses the Exodus from Egypt as a case in point and wonders how many children today would opt for the safe confines of slavery rather than risk the hardships of this defining event.

> Most of the Hebrew slaves in Pharaoh's Egypt could not imagine that they might successfully escape to freedom. Commentators on the biblical book of Exodus tell us that only twenty percent left to follow Moses. The rest stayed behind, enslaved by their fear for the unknown. The world in which we are raising our children challenges them with many straits and narrow places. We want them to have faith that they can make it through and leave the familiarity and safety of home. If we overprotect them, we enslave them with our fears. If we give them the freedom to develop strength through overcoming difficulties, they'll be out in front with the courageous twenty percent.[12]

Farther west, the twelve or thirteen year old will need to raise the level of adventure with more demanding physical activity like mountain biking, horse riding, canoeing or rock climbing. Sometimes the need to do this will be unspoken and it will be up to a parent to recognise this desire and offer encouragement and suggestions for new and exciting opportunities. At other times, our children will take the initiative.

For ten years, my wife and I worked at a summer institute in Maine. This was a fine arrangement for our family as it allowed us to leave the heat and humidity of Washington D.C. and spend six weeks in northern New England. From the time our daughter was four, we all headed north in July and our daughter took part in the programme that was provided for the children. In many ways, the environment there was ideal. The Steiner Institute was housed on a small college campus and my daughter and her special summer friends could safely walk anywhere on campus without restriction. It was a very different life from our suburban, car-oriented culture.

Just prior to her fourteenth birthday, our daughter began voicing reservations about returning to Maine. She complained that there was nothing to do. We reminded her that there were art classes, kayaking trips, beach excursions, innumerable opportunities provided by the children's programme, but she was adamant. So we began to explore other options. My wife did some research to find alternatives and discovered a wilderness canoe trip solely for teenage girls led by young women guides. The trip would be vigorous and rugged. The group would head off for a ten-day adventure with extensive paddling and portages. They would have to camp out, cook their own food, make do without the comforts of home (no showers, no toilets), and be at the mercy of the bugs and the weather. We were sure that our daughter would express no interest whatsoever. We were wrong. She wanted to go.

Sending her on this trip was a huge step for us. We had to leave her with her brother in Boston, knowing that she was getting on a plane for Canada and trusting that when she got off one of the tour leaders, whom we had never met, would be there to meet her. They would then journey six hours north of Toronto to the base camp where they would join the other girls and begin their trip. The only communication that we would have during the two weeks was a phone message that she had arrived in Toronto safely and two email messages — one when they left the base camp for their canoe trip and one when they returned.

At the end of the two weeks, my wife and I drove back to Boston eager to pick Ava up at the airport. When she came through customs, we were there waiting. She looked so pleased with herself, self-confident and mature. She was strong from the canoeing and portaging, healthy from the days out in the sun, and different, not just because of the hair rinse that the girls had shared on their adventure, but because she had completed a rite of passage.

The next year she was eager to return. She saved her baby-sitting money and spent nineteen days braving mosquitoes, white water, and the SARS epidemic. Sometimes, not protecting our children can be just as important as protecting them.

The Complaint Department

Everything becomes more vigorous west of the Missouri River. By the time we reach the Rockies and head into the last phase of childhood, complaining will likely have become an art form.

For parents of adolescents, complaining presents a significant challenge. We have to find ways to distinguish between those complaints that are genuine and justified and those that are simply part of the adolescent nature. Behind my daughter's complaints about returning with us to Maine was her wish to do something new and daring. That is why it is essential to listen carefully, reflect thoughtfully, seek the guidance of others, and always try to remember what we were like at that age.

One of my recurring memories from my own adolescence is how I complained bitterly to my parents about having to take part in family outings. The thought of being isolated in the company of my family seemed unbearable. I would fuss and express disbelief that I was being made to spend the whole day with them rather than with my friends. Oddly enough, the other part that I recall is that no matter what we did, I always had a great time. My memories of our recent family life with our two sons and our daughter also support this. The hardest part is getting underway. I have used these memories to help me recall that there are times when parents need to turn a deaf ear to their child's complaints and choose the activity that seems right for everyone.

Responsibilities

It is certainly true that complaining about family responsibilities will increase the farther west we go. No matter how well parents have instilled the habit of helping around the house, some amount of discontent is bound to arise.

As adolescent lives grow busier with commitments outside of the home, it becomes harder for parents to preserve time for household chores. Unfortunately, chores are usually the first activities to go when time becomes compressed. I say unfortunately because household responsibilities like leaf raking, house cleaning, and dishwashing teach our children lessons that are every bit as important as the ones they learn in school.

As we approach The Rocky Mountains of Childhood, we enter what may well be the most self-centred and self-involved period of our children's lives. This emerging sense of self makes adolescents feel like the focal point of all attention and leads them to spend hours in front of a mirror or on a cell phone or the computer instant messaging. It is a parent's responsibility at this time to help our children remember that life is a two-way street.

Maintaining household responsibilities at this age is crucial. I say 'maintaining' because chores need to be introduced around six and seven and increased in both size and difficulty as children mature. As adolescents begin to spend hours in the bathroom, it makes sense that they should do more to help keep it clean. As they begin to change their clothes repeatedly, it makes sense that they should help do the laundry. And when they eventually focus on learning to drive, which most young people do, then they can certainly help to maintain and clean the family car. All of these expectations are reasonable even though many children meet such expectations with ample amounts of disbelief.

As we ready our families for the ascent into the Rocky Mountains and the third and often most difficult part of the long journey, we should stop and take stock and make sure that we are prepared for this last phase of our trip. If we have been able to create emotional connectedness through the shared activities of family life and through a mild and temperate climate of love and respect, we will be better able to communicate with our children when challenges arise. And if we have been able to establish and maintain good habits and responsibilities, we will have helped to empower our children so that they can begin to chart their own course in the turbulent times ahead.

CHAPTER FIVE

Travelling in the Wild West

The Teenage Years

> When I was a boy of fourteen, my father was so ignorant
> I could hardly stand to have the old man around. But
> when I got to be twenty-one, I was astounded at how
> much he had learned in seven years.
>
> — MARK TWAIN, *Atlantic Monthly, 1874*

Parenting is usually a full-time job. But west of the Rockies, it will often seem like we are working overtime. Picture a school night. It's a little after ten and a mother has just settled down on the couch next to her son. His homework books are spread over the coffee table, a bag of crisps is on the floor, and the portable phone is on the arm of the couch. 'Why don't you pack up your things and get ready for bed?'

'Why? It's only 10:15,' the boy responds.

'There's school tomorrow and you have to get up early.'

'But I'm not tired. I'm going to stay up a little longer.'

The mother shakes her head and replies, 'No, you need your sleep. Remember you had a hard time getting up this morning.'

The son responds in frustration. 'Oh, come on. I didn't get up because I hate Mondays. It's my worst day of the week at school. Besides, it's early. No one in my class has to go to bed this early. You're the only parent that makes their kid go to bed before eleven. You know Alex stays up until midnight doing his homework. And so does Justin.'

'I am not their mother.'

'I know that. But why do I have to go to bed right now? It's not even ten-thirty. This is ridiculous.'

The mother stirs impatiently. She is finally sitting down for the first time all day and was hoping to relax with the newspaper. Now the conversation has become a debate.

'Look, you need more sleep than most kids and I just read in the paper that extended sleep is good for you. The amount of sleep you get before midnight directly affects your health. I want you to be healthy and I want you to get ready for bed.'

'You're so weird,' the boy responds, growing emotional. 'I don't need this much sleep. You treat me like I'm a baby. I'm surprised you don't ask me to rest after lunch. Why don't you let me grow up? If I go to bed now, I'm just going to lie there with my eyes open. Besides, if I get too much sleep, I'll be more tired in the morning.'

The mother smiles, 'If you get too much sleep, you'll be more tired in the morning? Please get ready for bed.'

'You are so strange. You're like the Amish.'

'I like the Amish,' the mother replies brightening. 'And I am weirder than your average mum. Keep in mind, in a couple of years you'll be going off to college and I won't know what time you go to bed. But as long as you're here, you'll have to remember three things. The first is that I love you, the second is that I'm weird, and the third is that you need your sleep. So please get up and get ready for bed.'

During the first two stages of childhood, from birth to grade one and from grade one to puberty, the active and emotional elements in a child's nature exert the greatest influence. But from the Rockies on, a third aspect will dominate. This will be the capacity for thinking. And from the moment that this important faculty for incisive, perceptive, and highly critical thinking starts to grow, arguments will multiply and all family policies and procedures will be open for inspection and discussion.

The development of critical thinking heralds another wave of increasing independence, one that often results in a marked separation between parents and children. This is a time when differences and distances between parents and children can widen as adult inconsistencies and flaws fall under the scrutiny of a young person's increasing critical awareness.

> At adolescence, the ties of believing discipleship are loosened. Attachment now is to the ideal rather than to persons. The youth is for this reason easily alienated from the actual personalities of parents and would-be teachers. He still longs to believe, but the persons who are available seldom prove worthy of belief . . .
>
> An adolescent finds his parents unworthy for what seem to be the slightest reasons! A characteristic mannerism, tone of voice, or attitude in his parents may turn his heart to stone and his will to fire against them. For him these trivialities are not trivial. They are the clear evidence of bigoted, sterile, untrue, or otherwise objectionable elements in his parents' thoughts and feelings. The least hint of these elements in their manner reminds the young person of all that he has suffered from the character that lies behind the manner. His intimacy with this unwanted trait makes him reject it the more violently. It is not only bad: it is already in his own blood. We spurn an external noisomeness; but we are beside ourselves with repulsion if the unwholesome thing is discovered clinging to our person.[13]

In an effort to separate from their parents and begin to stand on their own, young people argue against the very beliefs that have shaped them from day one. This resistance is expressed in different ways. The quiet, thoughtful child does it subtly with looks of displeasure and well-timed remarks. The light-hearted child does it with a smile, obliviousness, and growing irreverence. And the alpha child does it with verve and swagger.

Although this can mark the beginning of the most challenging time in the parent-child relationship, it is also a necessary stage of development. The onset of the teenage years form childhood's Continental Divide. Parents should note this juncture on the map. As it was for the early pioneers, from this point on, the journey can become a matter of survival.

When we reach the Rocky Mountains and enter the last third of the country, the surroundings are more dramatic than anything we have seen previously. The landscape is spectacular. Like the teenage years, this is a region of extremes, both with regard to weather and terrain. In a matter of hours, we can go from the highest mountain in the continental United States, Mount Whitney, 4267 metres (14,000 feet) above sea level, to the lowest point below sea level, Death Valley. And the temperature can vary by as much as 21° C (70° F) — often just how life is with a teenager.

The Rockies provide a magnificent entryway to this region, jagged and snow-covered. From a distance they are splendid to behold. But high up in those mountains, above the treeline and the snowline, where the ponds are milky and cold from glacial runoff and strong winds blow continuously, we can be left with the distinct impression that we are not welcome.

Scott Russell Sanders has captured this experience in his insightful book, *Hunting for Hope: A Father's Journeys.*

> On a June morning high in the Rocky Mountains of Colorado, snowy peaks rose before me like the promise of a world without grief. A creek full of melt-water roiled along to my left, and to my right an aspen grove shimmered with new leaves. Bluebirds darted in

and out of holes in the aspen trunks and butterflies flickered beside every puddle . . .

With all of that to look at, I gazed instead at my son's broad back as he stalked away from me up the trail. Sweat had darkened his gray T-shirt in patches the colour of bruises. His shoulders were stiff with anger that would weight his tongue and keep his face turned from me for hours. Anger had also made him quicken his stride, gear after gear, until I could no longer keep up . . .

For the previous year or so, no matter how long our spells of serenity, Jesse and I had kept falling into quarrels, like victims of malaria breaking out in fever. We might be talking about soccer or supper, about the car keys or the news, and suddenly our voices would begin to clash like swords. I had proposed this trip to the mountains in hopes of discovering the source of that strife.

The peace between us held until we turned back from the waterfall and began discussing where to camp the following night. Jesse wanted to push on up to Thunder Lake, near eleven thousand feet, and pitch our tent on snow. I wanted to stop a thousand feet lower and sleep on dry dirt.

'We're not equipped for snow,' I told him.

'Sure we are. Why do you think I bought a new sleeping bag? Why did I call ahead to reserve snow-shoes?'

I suggested that we could hike up from a lower campsite and snowshoe to our hearts content.

He loosed a snort of disgust. 'I can't believe you're wimping out on me, Dad.'

'I'm just being sensible.'

'You're wimping out. I came here to see the

backcountry and all you want to do is poke around the foothills.'

'This isn't wild enough for you?' I waved my arms at the view. 'What do you need — avalanches and grizzlies?'

Just then, as we rounded a bend, an elderly couple came shuffling toward us, hunched over walking sticks, white hair jutting from beneath their straw hats. They were followed by three toddling children, each rigged out with tiny backpack and canteen. Jesse and I stood aside to let them pass, returning nods to their cheery hellos.

After they had trooped by, Jesse muttered, 'We're in the wilds, huh, Dad? That's why the trail's full of grandparents and kids.' Then he quickened his pace until the damp blond curls that dangled below his billed cap were slapping against his neck.

'Is this how it's going to be?' I called after him. 'You're going to spoil the trip because I won't agree to camp on snow?'

He turned and glared at me. 'You're the one who's spoiling it, you and your hang-ups. You always ruin everything.[14]

Communication — Deserts and Glaciers

Communicating with teenagers can be a challenging experience, marked by icy chasms and barren desert-like stretches. Both boys and girls can be particularly difficult to converse with at this age. An intense urge for privacy causes our children to store up their experiences. Even those children who were quite outgoing when they were younger may rarely speak to their parents about the things that are most on their mind.

For this reason, fostering communication is essential. One of the primary objectives for parents is to know what their teenager thinks. Without conversation and communication, this will be difficult to ascertain. And without regularly recurring opportunities, conversation and real communication won't happen.

Probably the most obvious place for conversations to take place is the dinner table. It is one venue where parents and children can meet in a predictable way, a way that hopefully has been firmly established in both of the first two phases in childhood.

However, even something seemingly as common as eating dinner together has become an uncommon occurrence in the lives of many American families. Especially during the teenage years, the busy schedule of events makes it challenging for families to find regular times to eat together in a relaxed way, the kind of undisturbed gathering that allows conversation to develop naturally. But dinnertime should be one of the sacred spaces in family life, protected from interruptions and distractions. And even if dinnertime isn't the place where we have our most important conversations, it is surely the place where we maintain and service the lines of communication between our children and ourselves.

It is so important to establish good habits in the early years by example. If we regularly jump up from the dinner table to answer the phone, we will establish a precedent that will make it nearly impossible to have meaningful encounters around the dinner table during the teenage years. The ordering of life must start early on before the entropy of adolescence begins. If we have omitted family routines and rituals, we will discover during the teenage years that we lack opportunities to connect with our children. And it will be very difficult to create these anew in this last stage of childhood. But if we have regularly eaten dinner as a family and spoken with each other in an interested and caring way, this kind of interaction will be the norm and as such, it will be more easily maintained.

Although dinnertime is an important family routine, in and of itself, it will not facilitate all of the communication that is necessary. Some teenagers will listen, laugh, and even linger at the table, but they won't necessarily share what's on their mind. Every parent must be on the look out for those times when their children are more likely to speak openly.

One mother that I spoke with said that when her daughter was a teenager, she realized that the best way to find out about her day was to say nothing. For weeks, she had tried greeting her daughter with the customary question, 'How was your day?' and got no response. So she changed her approach. When her daughter came home from high school, she didn't say much, she just put a nice snack on the table and continued to putter around in the kitchen. Her daughter would sit down at the table and start to eat and before long she was telling her mother everything about her day. The mum kept 'working,' seemingly occupied by other things, but really she was listening as closely as she could to everything her daughter said.

All teenagers have times when they are more likely to talk. Most often those times occur when we are standing side by side rather than conversing face to face. Some children talk more in the car and some, like my second son, talk most when they drive. He wouldn't say much at the dinner table, but if you handed him the keys to the car, especially on a long trip, he would settle in behind the wheel and talk about everything that was going on in his life.

Other adolescents will open up at odd hours. Parents who wait up for their children at the weekend not only see if they come home on time but often find that the late hours are conducive to conversation. A teenager's weekend biorhythm is significantly different than a parent's and often he or she will just begin to wind down around eleven and be more open to reflect on the events of the day. Many important conversations occur after hours.

Having friends over to the house also will help us to know what our own child is thinking.

> The families of teenagers that work the best usually
> have an open door to their house (and refrigerator).
> A free flow of young people, friends, family, and
> neighbors fosters the kind of stimulating atmosphere

that helps teenagers feel at ease and open up. Through the conversations that arise naturally, through both speaking and listening, young people explore what they think.[15]

Our family friends and relatives who visit our homes often have better success at eliciting responses to important questions than we do. Many times parents will be surprised to hear what their child adds to these discussions. Unexpected thoughts and opinions will surface.

For any of these opportunities to yield free and interesting conversation, there must be a prevailing atmosphere of respect for what young people think. Our children are developing their thinking faculties west of the Rockies, but this is a work in progress, one that will take quite a while to complete. It is a parent's responsibility to assist this process through conversation and interest. We are not called on to be teachers in this dialogue, but learners. It is our assignment to find out what and how our children think. We should try to help our children clarify their thinking, but not correct it. Teenagers will change their minds repeatedly from the Rockies all the way to the Pacific Ocean. Our hope should be that at the end of this journey, they will be able think for themselves. To realize this hope, we will have to be prepared to help them explore some challenging topics and endure a fair amount of provocation.

One young fellow that I know took pleasure in provoking his father with his hair styles. His dad is a quiet, kind, but fairly traditional man. So the son decided to challenge his values emphatically by getting a Mohawk haircut. He told me that when he got his hair cut, he went home at dinnertime and walked into the kitchen, focusing on his father's reaction. Although his father restrained himself and said nothing, his son saw the expression on his face tighten.

'Something the matter, Dad?' he asked, trying to goad a response.

'No,' the father replied.

Perhaps the father was adhering to the old saying, 'If you can't say something nice, it is better to say nothing at all.' Yet, the son was clearly disappointed by his father's unwillingness to confront this issue.

Teenagers often gravitate toward shock value and hyperbole. They will raise a basic question such as: 'Who am I?' in a dramatic manner, trying to elicit an honest response by unsettling us. At these moments, they provide us with an opportunity to clarify the complicated issue of whether who they are is determined by character traits such as warm heartedness, integrity, and responsibility or by physical characteristics, such as body-piercing, ripped clothing, and hair colour.

This is an interesting question to explore as an abstraction, but far more challenging when it is raised provocatively right in our home and perhaps when we least expect it. Teenagers often pose their important questions in emotionally charged atmospheres. They may pick a family reunion as the time to shave their head or pierce their nose, knowing on some level that this emotionally charged situation will make this learning experience that much more memorable. If we respond emotionally, trouble awaits us. But if we have the wherewithal to maintain a calm and reasonable demeanour, the conversation that results can be a significant opportunity for growth for everyone involved.

Recently I was visiting a small private school (for children aged 5–18) during an open house for grandparents. This was an annual spring event. It was a special day for the younger children and especially for the grandparents who visited the classrooms and saw some performances by the children in the auditorium.

As it turned out, it was also a day when one of the high school seniors decided to test the school's dress code by showing up in full drag. He borrowed his girl friend's tight red dress, her makeup, her stockings, her bra, and her purse and walked into school. He is a bright and attractive guy, who later said that he was just questioning the validity of the school's dress code. But he also knowingly put his school and the school administrators in a difficult position. He knew that if the school asked him to leave, it would be perceived by the student body as being reactionary. And if they let him stay at school, it would shock many of the grandparents who would worry about the kind of school their grandchildren were attending.

It was truly a challenge and an opportunity at the same time, the kind that can either bring out our best or our worst. As I listened in on the discussion between the high school administrator and this student, I grew more and more impressed. The administrator sat with him in her office and calmly and painstakingly explored the issues he was trying to raise. She respected his thinking but also challenged it and was able through her questions to bring some of his inconsistencies to light.

'Yes,' she said, 'This is a good question to raise in the high school student body. But it would have been better if you had shown up dressed like this for the whole-high-school forum two days ago. That would have been the perfect place to bring this issue to the attention of your fellow students. But the grandparents do not need to take up this question.'

I felt this was the perfect response to this student. He was raising a complex and difficult question, and the way to respond was through clear and calm thinking. If she had reacted emotionally, the situation would have deteriorated rapidly and become polarized. She would have eliminated any opportunity to learn from the situation. But through serious, intelligent and probing discussion, she was able to represent the school and assist the student at the same time.

This is a reminder that when difficult situations arise with our teenagers, it is essential that we speak calmly, however difficult it may be to do so in the heat of the moment. When we are annoyed and angry, our chances of having a positive conversation diminish dramatically. It is probably wise to postpone any discussion until we cool down. Sometimes holding a family meeting after dinner is the perfect solution.

Whenever I offer workshops for parents and particularly for fathers, I like to have the participants recall those moments when their relationship with their own parents was severely tested. More often than not, they recall situations that involved the tensions that arise when teenagers start to question their parents' assumptions and begin to think for themselves. Though this can be a difficult, emotionally challenging time for parents, it is developmentally appropriate behaviour for teenagers — it is how they move to being independent, thinking adults. In this last phase of childhood, parents need to focus on thinking as strongly as they focused on activity and feeling during the first and second phases. Though it is not always easy, I invariably urge parents to respect and understand their children's thinking.

But having said this, I must also add that there is a difference between a teenager thinking on his own and acting on his own, especially when safety, health, or morality is involved. For example, a child may think that driving at high speeds would be an exhilarating experience. There are even many adults who feel that way. Although I am not one, I can accept that some intelligent, reasonable human beings like to drive fast. I also accept the fact that a child of mine might concur with this notion. Still, it is my responsibility to let my children know that regardless of what they think, while they live at home and drive the family car, they are not to drive at high speeds. Perhaps, as adults, they will pursue this interest and drive race cars on a race track at death defying speeds. That would be worrisome to me, but really, at a certain point, it is their choice. But for young people still living at home, there sometimes needs to be a distinction between what they think and what they do. It is my responsibility as a parent to make this distinction clear.

In a recent article in *The Washington Post*, Sarah Brown, head of the National Campaign to Prevent Teen Pregnancy, addressed this issue with a balanced perspective.

> Talking to your kids is absolutely essential. But it is also absolutely insufficient. Two decades of top-notch research . . . clearly show that it is the overall depth and texture of relationships ('connections') between parents and kids that make all the difference. This research also shows that setting fair limits and expectations — and enforcing them — is critical.[16]

Family Meetings

> I have come to feel that probably no single structure
> will help you prioritize your family more than a
> specific time set aside every week just for the family.
> You could call it 'family time,' 'family hour,' 'family
> council,' or 'family night' if you prefer . . . On a typical
> family night we would review the calendar on upcom-
> ing events so everyone would know what was going
> on. Then we'd hold a family council and discuss issues
> and problems. We'd give each other suggestions, and
> together we would discuss issues and problems . . .'[17]

— STEVEN COVEY, *7 Habits of Highly Successful Families*

Family meetings can be so effective with adolescents and teenagers that many parents schedule them regularly. They provide an opportunity to talk about the upcoming week's schedule, transportation arrangements, and any joint work projects that are planned for the week or weekend, as well as a chance to see if our young people have any concerns or need any help.

Family meetings also provide a time to address the difficult situations. Families can always schedule 'emergency' family meetings to speak about more serious concerns, but usually it is best if difficulties can be anticipated and addressed in the normal course of the family routine in a timely way.

My experience is that teenagers do not usually act out in isolated and unexpected ways. Rather I think their challenging behaviours develop incrementally. If small problems are addressed in a timely way they often subside. But if they are not adequately responded to, they can culminate in a more dramatic incident. Let me give an example. In one family, the oldest son was a senior in high school. During his last year at home, he began to make his own transition to college. He had his own car, a part-time job, and a fair amount of independence. Like most teenagers, he lived into this new independence with enthusiasm and started to test the limits of his newfound freedom. He stayed out late, skipped dinner at home to be at his girlfriend's house, and began to do his homework assignments in spurts, leaving schoolwork until the last minute rather than doing it regularly each night as he had in the past. This is, of course, the way many college students operate. They stay up late, work in sporadic bursts, and live it up. This young fellow was adopting the college model a year early.

When this type of behaviour happens at college, parents don't usually know. If their son or daughter is able to successfully complete course work and maintain good grades and good health, parents may never find out. But when young people living at home noticeably alter their routines, parents can become uneasy and confused. We see our son or daughter getting older and know that soon he or she will be in college. Even though our intuitions are telling us the current situation is not right, instead of confronting them, we often question ourselves. We might wonder if we are having trouble letting go and allowing our child to make decisions on his or her own. In this particular situation, the parents were both uneasy and unsure and so they said nothing.

Then, one night their son was coming home late from his girlfriend's house. He was hurrying because he was out after his curfew and because he was driving later than he could legally drive in his state at the age of seventeen. On his way home, his car skidded through a stop sign on wet leaves and hit another car. Fortunately, no one was seriously injured, but the boy was taken to the hospital for an examination and given citations for failing to stop at a stop sign and for driving after curfew.

When the son called on his cell phone to tell his parents about the accident, they were upset. Once they realized that he was not injured, they responded strongly as parents are likely to do when they have been frightened and had their lingering worries confirmed. However, this event didn't just happen. It had been building for several weeks. The parents had felt uneasy about their son's behaviour and yet had not found a way to address the problem. The accident was essentially the dramatic and dangerous culmination of an extended series of increasingly troubling behaviours.

Regular family meetings help parents address these kinds of problems before they reach this crisis stage. These meetings provide two important ways to communicate and connect. The first is a consistent, non-threatening and non-confrontational time to discuss problem areas before they become a crisis. The second is a regular opportunity to reflect and assess the health of our family. Knowing that we are going to sit down for a regular Sunday or Monday evening meeting helps us to be more conscious of difficult situations. If we parent as part of a team, we have the added benefit of being able to ask our spouse for his or her assessment of the situation ahead of time. The conversations that take place privately between a mother and a father prior to the family meetings can be just as important as the conversations that take place in the meetings.

Family meetings with teens should address problems clearly, concretely, and succinctly, but they should also accent the positive. At some part of the meeting, parents need to show that they have not failed to notice, nor taken for granted, the many good things their children do.

Family meetings should not be too long, but they should always allow time for discussions and differences of opinion. These gatherings play an important role in fostering communication because they address divisive issues in an atmosphere of respect. Not all family meetings in our house achieved the desired level of respectful, reasonable discourse. But that was always our goal and when it was achieved, my wife and I cheered inwardly.

Two-Way Traffic

Family meetings also help our teenagers learn an essential lesson: *Life is a two-way street*. American teenagers have grown increasingly self-centred and demanding, adopting a strong sense of entitlement. This understanding is reflected in popular parenting books like *Get Out of My Life, But First Drive Cheryl and Me to the Mall: A Parent's Guide to the New Teenager.* Balancing this self-centred tendency by preserving and cultivating an awareness of others is another of the important lessons that families provide.

Raising healthy teenagers is an arduous task, but it is not so complicated as it sometimes seems. In an excellent and insightful parenting book, *Too Much of a Good Thing: Raising Children of Character in an Indulgent Age*, Dan Kindlon describes the results of a survey given to 639 teenagers. In this survey he discovered 81 young people (approximately 12%) who seemed problem free.

> They didn't drink, smoke cigarettes or marijuana; they weren't depressed, mean, spoiled, or self-centred; they didn't suffer from eating problems; they said it was wrong for thirteen-year olds to have sex; and they worked to their intellectual potential in school without being overly driven. What separated these too-good-to-be-true teens from their peers? According to [the] data, five things: their families frequently ate dinner together, their parents were not divorced or separated, they had to keep their rooms clean, they didn't have a phone in their room, and they did community service.[18]

What these findings show is that healthy families raise healthy children. It is important to add that there are many healthy, adjusted teenagers who have been raised by single mums and single dads, parents completely dedicated to raising healthy, productive children. Perhaps the key word in parenting is dedicated. To achieve even the simplest objectives like eating dinner together or seeing that children keep their rooms clean, parents will need persistent focus, unwavering commitment, and a fairly thick skin.

Volcanic Eruptions and Emotional Outbursts

> You have to understand. I am under so much stress with homework and tryouts. It just makes me feel better when I scream at someone. You're my parents. If I can't scream at you, who can I scream at?
>
> — A HIGH SCHOOL FRESHMAN

There really isn't a way to be an effective parent and to make our teenager happy all of the time. If we are going to ask our young people to be responsible, to have a regular curfew, to avoid parties without adult supervision, to take part in family gatherings, we are going to encounter seismic activity. Emotional outbursts are common during the teenage years, especially for young people who live life with intensity. Although our teenagers have entered the last phase of childhood, where thinking plays a more dominant role, strong feelings still abound. It is important for our teens to have legitimate and appropriate ways to express the strong feelings that are swirling inside so that they don't make a habit out of being rude and disrespectful to those closest to them.

The Healing Power of Art

> Browns, blacks, and dark reds streak the canvas-deep colours, abstract forms swimming into focus, painted in thick angry strokes. Angela has been at it now for five hours non-stop, venting, her black-handled brush a blur. It is three in the morning, the house silent as a crypt, except for the hollow, sandy sound of sable

on canvas, almost like breathing. School — her senior year — has barely started, but she is as stressed as if it were the finals week. Only the painting helps, keeps her hands from trembling, the tears from flowing. She is already on her second canvas.

— EDWARD HUMES, *School of Dreams*

One of the best ways that young people can appropriately express their feelings is through art. If teenagers dance, paint, draw, act, sing, or play a musical instrument, they have outlets to express their strong feelings in healthy ways. Art and music have the added attraction of providing young people with an opportunity to express their intense and confusing feelings non-verbally. When our teens are given these artistic opportunities regularly through the high school curriculum or through extra-curricular activities, they are provided with the safety valve they need to let off emotional steam before it builds up, causing explosive situations.

Ironically, young people at this age are often prone to give up the artistic activity that they have been involved with for years, just when it would serve them best. The discipline — the perseverance required to be truly accomplished — can present a considerable challenge for youth. If parents are sensitive to this challenge and yet recognise the value of having a creative outlet, they can work creatively to encourage continued artistic activity.

In our family, the key was finding the right music teacher. Unfortunately she did not live close by. Each week my wife or I would drive for nearly an hour to Baltimore to take our daughter to her music lesson. However, it was worth the inconvenience. Her enthusiasm for playing her viola deepened along with her growing fondness and respect for her new teacher. And we all benefitted by having time for many important conversations on those long drives.

The San Andreas Fault: When the Ground We Stand Upon Is Shaken.

During the third phase of the parenting journey, the ground beneath our feet will seem less certain. Our young people will demonstrate sudden dramatic shifts in attitude and behaviour and these shifts will at times leave us bewildered and unsteady. The stress of parenting in the third phase of childhood may cause us to lose sight of the fact that the simple principles that guided us in our parenting of younger children are still important in the lives of teenagers. These same ideals need to be continually interwoven in the life of the teenager because they promote health, and healthy, well-rounded teenagers are far less likely to be in crisis.

In her fine book, *The Shelter of Each Other: Rebuilding Families*, Mary Pipher describes various families of teenagers in crisis that she has seen in her practice. As a therapist, she has addressed the problems that these young people face — such as drug and alcohol abuse, premature and prolonged sexual activity, truancy, and despondency — with simple recommendations that foster basic emotional, physical, and mental health. She has repeatedly encouraged families to spend uninterrupted time together regularly without technology (TV, CD players, video games, Internet, cell phones, etc.), to be out in nature regularly, and to eat meals together. She has found that these simple suggestions help families turn back in the right direction, diminish discipline issues, and promote better parent-child relations.

It is in this third phase of childhood that we will need to continue to foster a well-balanced home-life, one that keeps our children physically, emotionally, and mentally active. Young people have an unvoiced longing which can best be expressed by the following words of Ralph Waldo Emerson: 'The one thing which we seek with insatiable desire is to forget ourselves, to be surprised out of our propriety . . . and to do something without knowing how or why; in short to draw a new circle.' Our young people should be encouraged to pursue their interests. Anything that moves the focus of their attention away from themselves and expands the circumference of their world provides a welcome balance. When these interests elicit a passionate response, we can be reassured that their feelings are engaged as well. If this emotional involvement propels our children into positive action, gets them off the couch, out of the bedroom, and into contact with others, new friendships will form and their world will expand in a good way.

It goes without saying that we should be interested in the hobbies, books, organizations, and issues that interest our children. These matters engage our children's thinking and enable their knowledge of the world to expand rapidly in surprising ways during these latter years.

Sometimes parents need help and a little luck in making this happen. My fifteen-year-old daughter plays each week with the Washington D.C. Youth Orchestra. Her mother or I faithfully drive her to these rehearsals early on Saturday morning and pick her up hours later. But frankly, I don't think we ever could have persuaded her to give up sleeping in on Saturday morning so she could play her viola with 75 teenage musicians whom she had never met before. Fortunately, her music teacher convinced her to take part. And it turns out that the D.C. Youth Orchestra has been one of the best experiences for her. Her enthusiasm for playing the viola has grown along with her knowledge and skill. In addition, the companionship of her fellow musicians in the orchestra, in her section, and in her ensemble, has sustained her, and her interactions with her new circle of friends has given her new confidence. In short, she has drawn a new circle.

Another important piece in the life of a healthy teenager is activity. Young people need activity in the teenage years as much as they needed it during the first two phases of childhood.

At a parenting conference in Toronto, a father of a teenager asked me what he could do to reconnect with his son. Their father-son relationship had been severely strained over the past year and the father had come to our seminar seeking help. In an effort to assist him, I asked him to describe the last time that he and his son had met on really good terms. His response was very instructive. He said that a while back he had decided to pave his driveway and invited some of his friends over to help. His son had joined them to take part in the work. The father described how happy his son was working, perspiring, and eating lunch with the other men as an equal. This story was a lesson to all of us in the room. It was a reminder that two key ingredients in raising healthy teenagers are purposeful, challenging activities and meaningful contact with adults in situations of responsibility.

Every teenager longs for this rite of passage, for the recognition that they are no longer a child. This experience comes most easily through active, purposeful work. There are a variety of benefits in being an active teenager. Studies show that the chemicals secreted by our bodies during physical exertion, like serotonin or endorphins, help to improve our moods and our outlook. Physical activity is a sound preventive remedy for the increase in teenage depression. We know, as well, that as a country we need to be concerned over the increasing rate of obesity and it is well known that activity helps to reduce appetite and nervous eating as well as increase metabolism. On both a physical and an emotional level, activity is beneficial.

When teenagers' regular purposeful activity intertwines with their interests and fosters emotional involvement through social interactions and heartfelt participation, we have an unbeatable combination, one that will leave our young people feeling good about themselves. And when teenagers feel good about themselves, they are less likely to act in ways that lead to severe disciplinary situations.

It is, however, worth mentioning again that even healthy children are not problem-free. West of the Rockies, the land is as varied as it is beautiful. There are still numerous peaks and valleys, all sorts of extremes. There are vast stretches of desert and deep green temperate rainforests. There is the pale barrenness of the Great Salt Lake and the Bonneville Salt Flats and the earthy red tones of the Colorado River and the Grand Canyon. This is a region that is both austere and exquisitely beautiful, and California is still to come.

California — The Promised Land of College

For many parents, college will be the place where the third phase of our parenting draws to a close in much the same way that arriving in California signals the culmination of our journey across the country. College life offers many of the appealing characteristics associated with the Golden State. It is a place where the sun seems to shine more brightly, where everyone is more laid back, and where traffic just seems to stop the moment you step into the street. College can be as wild or superficial as Hollywood, as progressive as Berkeley, or as charming as San Francisco. Seeing it now in hindsight, as a parent, it seems like a most luxurious time — not just because it costs so much, but because it provides young people with an extraordinary opportunity to expand their thinking and to learn about the world and about themselves.

Although our parenting journey does not end with college orientation or the start of classes, our level of parental involvement will depend on our individual child. As Dan Kindlon pointed out in *Too Much of a Good Thing*, sometimes one of our children will be like a Mercedes Benz, stable and dependable, while another child will be more like an MG sports car — exciting, but subject to breakdowns.[19]

My oldest son was the dependable Mercedes. Like the typical first child, he was eager to begin college and throughout his college years, he required little maintenance. He received a scholarship, maintained a 'B+' average to keep his scholarship, applied for overseas study (and funding), had several jobs, and ended up being a hall-director, which afforded him free room and board. He was easy and there was little that we, as parents, had to do.

His brother, on the other hand, raised in the same family and under the same circumstances, was a completely different story. We have a photo of him outside his dormitory on the day that we drove him to college for his freshmen year. I can see now that he looks fearful and uncertain to be on his own. His college experience required much more attention and even some intervention.

In October of his junior year, he decided to take a twelve-hour overnight train trip from Cleveland, Ohio, to Portland, Maine, so that he could then catch a Greyhound bus to visit his old girlfriend at her college. I remember wondering why he would spend two of the five days he had for fall break on a train, especially when he also had a serious amount of course work that was due when he returned. Well, six days later, he returned to school late, exhausted, and sick with a serious amount of course work still to do. It was then that he called home to say that he was not sure that 'college was for him' and he was thinking of taking a leave of absence.

By this time I had finally come to understand that when he said that he was thinking about doing something, it was imminent. I knew that I needed to do damage control and so I got on a plane and flew to Cleveland, rented a car, and drove down to his college. It was a good and important visit. We talked about school. We worked over his outline for a major research project. I met with one of his professors to see what he would recommend. We ate meals together and watched the World Series in my hotel room. He stayed in school and eventually graduated with his class.

For me, this was uncharted territory on the parenting journey. It was new and hazardous. When we made it through, I felt good about my parenting, and the words of Yogi Berra had new meaning: 'It ain't over 'til it's over.'

Parenting at the end of our coast to coast journey requires a fine blend of attentiveness and restraint. College offers young people an opportunity to stand on their own and to put their talents and abilities to the test. Independence is the fifth course they take each semester and it is certainly their split major. Part of the required material in that course of study is learning from mistakes. It is not our job as parents to prevent all mistakes. Balancing a chequebook, paying a phone bill, learning to budget money and time, and being responsible with work-study commitments is our child's responsibility. When they master this course work, they grow up. Our job is to be attentive, to watch for the signs of health, and sometimes to help with disaster relief. But if we do too much for our children, even if it is out of kindness, we do not serve them well.

Each year of college brings our children closer to the end of the journey and somewhere around the age of 21, our children should have acquired confidence in their ability to direct their own lives. Even the high maintenance college students, the ones for whom regular phone calls, e-mails and periodic visits and care packages are a must, seem to find their bearing for the last year of college. Somewhere in their senior year, young people start to see the Pacific Ocean through the thinning trees of the western forests. Whether it is along the coast at Point Reyes, Muir Woods, Golden Gate Park, or Big Sur, the ocean becomes visible in the distance before they ever set foot on the beach. This sense of having arrived fills our young people with promise and fills us with mixed emotions. Our parenting journey is coming to an end.

I don't remember my sons' college graduations as sad events. The ceremonies were quietly joyful and filled with a sense of accomplishment, especially for my wife and me when we realized that we had actually sent two of our children to college on our meagre income. But the truth is, these graduations marked the end of an era. Our oldest son took a job in Atlanta after college and in the years that followed, met his wife, started a family, and bought a house there. Our second son took a job in Boston, met his fiancée and is now settled with his new work in his new city. We see too little of either of them. College marked the beginning of the end. It was on the map right from the start, but even after such a long journey, it seemed to come too soon.

CHAPTER SIX

The Challenge of Driving

Together and Alone

The course of true love is never smooth.

-WILLIAM SHAKESPEARE

Any cross-country trip can have its mishaps with detours and breakdowns, places where all forward progress stops and tensions rise. It is no different with parenting. Husbands and wives start out on their parenting journey offering each other the promise of companionship and support. But in actuality marriage ends up being its own demanding course of study, with challenging upper level classes in human nature, conflict resolution, and learning to live with opposites.

A charming movie from India, *Monsoon Wedding*, provides a fine example of some of the course material. In one very telling scene, the father and the mother of the bride begin a discussion about their youngest child's future. In the father's eyes, his young teenage son is adrift. He has no structure in his life to direct him and, much to the father's dismay, spends most of his time watching the cooking channel on television and is actually thinking of becoming a chef.

The father is disturbed by his son's lack of focus and wants to instill structure in his child's life through a rigorous boarding school environment. The father believes that if his son is given this external structure and discipline, he will shape up and grow up, begin to develop purposefulness and focus, and hopefully become something accomplished like an engineer.

The mother, on the other hand, has the opposite point of view. Her son is still her little boy who needs understanding and support so that his talents and interests can unfold slowly from within. She resists the ready answer of external structure because it is insensitive and wants instead to provide understanding and love.

The mother's position is based on an inner approach — loving understanding. The father's position is based on an external one — structure and firmness. The two positions are opposites and the conversation quickly becomes oppositional, leaving both the mother and father convinced that the other parent couldn't be more wrong.

Although the circumstances and the positions can vary from family to family, this is a common parenting scenario — one that typically ends in frustration and distance. Yet it doesn't have to be that way. In this case, the two parents could easily have concluded that they were both right. Loving understanding and firmness are opposite parenting approaches, but they are not exclusive. Without both of these polarities there is no wholeness. Firmness without loving understanding can be harsh and insensitive and loving understanding without firmness can be permissive and indulgent. But blended together these two points of view become loving firmness, clearly the most balanced approach to discipline.

To parent effectively, husbands and wives need to learn to embrace their differences and blend opposites. The complexity and worthiness of this undertaking is underscored in a remarkable way by E.F. Schumacher:

> Through all our lives we are faced with the task of
> reconciling opposites which, in logical thought, cannot
> be reconciled . . . How can one reconcile the demands
> of freedom and discipline in education? Countless
> mothers and teachers, in fact, do it, but no one can
> write down a solution. They do it by bringing into the
> situation a force that belongs to a higher level where
> opposites are transcended — the power of love. . . .
> Divergent problems force us to strain ourselves; they
> demand and thus provoke the supply of forces from a
> higher level, thus bringing love, beauty, goodness and
> truth into our lives. It is only with the help of these
> higher forces that opposites can be reconciled in the
> living situation.[20]

Responsibility and freedom, continuity and spontaneity, work and play are
just some of the opposites that need to be blended together in family life. But
there is no recipe that tells us how to blend opposites and how often. You simply
have to be fully present in the moment to sense the right proportion. That is
why good parenting is an art. In fact, parenting is a particularly challenging art
form because it is not created in the peaceful confines of a studio, at a writing
desk, on a piano, or in a quiet pastoral setting with paints and an easel. Instead,
the art of parenting develops on the school-run on a rainy morning or in the
kitchen before dinner when everyone is hungry. And to make matters even more
complicated, many of us create this art form working in tandem like Rogers and
Hammerstein or Lennon and McCartney although at times it feels more like
Abbot and Costello.

There are many hard jobs and parenting is one of the hardest. Parenting as
a couple and maintaining a relationship is harder still. No matter how com-
patible we are when we begin our relationship, as we age we become set in
our ways. Tendencies and dispositions become pronounced and predictable,
inspiring in our partners a growing desire for balance.

My neighbour is an excellent carpenter, one of the best I've seen. I am
convinced that he can make anything with wood. For him, every project

is a creation offering unlimited variations and possibilities. For this reason, his work is open ended and the creative process matters most of all. A while back, his wife asked him to put up a fence around their house. He gave considerable thought to the design, the materials, the suppliers, the hardware, all number of considerations that would influence his work. As he deliberated and considered the possibilities for an extended period of time, his wife worried about her children and grew impatient; so she went out and hired a fence company to do the job. As her husband became more involved in the process, she became more and more goal oriented.

A couple of years ago, I was asked to give a talk on the challenges of co-parenting. I titled it, 'Mothering and Fathering: Can We Really Do This Work Together?' In that talk, I tried to focus in part on a question that comes up repeatedly in so many families. 'Are we talking about the same child?' Parents often see their children and their children's needs in strikingly different ways. In order to do our parenting work together, we have to find a way to blend our divergent points of view and see them as complementary rather than oppositional.

Both marriage and parenting are transformational undertakings. To successfully grow and work together, it is essential that we remain open to learning. In particular, we have to be willing to learn from our spouse. Contained in their perspective is a point of view that completes and enhances our own.

In order for husbands and wives to learn from each other, however, there must be time for uninterrupted conversations. That is one of the reasons that I believe that children should go to bed early. Fathers and mothers need to have time to talk privately about the children so that they can create a shared picture of their children's needs and their parenting objectives. If this doesn't happen, our parenting approaches can become incompatible and we will end up working against each other. It is also important that these conversations take place regularly each week so that on those rare occasions when we get a babysitter and have time to go out for dinner alone, we don't end up talking about the children, but instead enjoy each other's company.

Friends of ours have four young children and any visit to their home provides an immediate reminder of how much time, energy, and focused attention it takes to raise a large family. These parents do a fine job with their children, but they also do an excellent job of tending their marriage. I don't know many couples with four children but I can easily say that these two individuals have as warm and vibrant a relationship as any I see. One of their secrets is making sure that they have time together as a couple. Because their children go to bed before eight, they have time in the evening to get together twice each week. One meeting is for business — bills, appointments, concerns about the children, etc. The second meeting is just for fun, no difficult issues are allowed. They may talk about the children on these occasions, but the testier issues are avoided. What matters most is that they set aside this one time each week for nurturing their marriage.

The fact is that our children's needs are nearly endless and they can easily consume us and obscure the needs of our relationship to our spouse. It is often the case that the very thing that caused us to start our family — a warm, loving relationship — goes untended amidst the responsibilities of work, home, and school.

Recently a friend of ours sent her third and youngest daughter off to college. We wondered if it would be hard for this wonderfully dedicated mother to find her house empty and all her children gone. When we saw her the other day, my wife asked (with a little trepidation) how she was doing. She replied, 'Great! As long as the girls were home,' she said, 'they came first. But now that they are gone, Eddie and I are spending time together talking about history and science and all kinds of things. It's wonderful!'

Marriages need tending. They require time, attention, and on occasion, hard work, but they also have so much to give. In a strong, healthy marriage, which is not by any means a problem-free marriage, we often find the essential piece that we need to be good partners and good parents.

For years, I thought that falling in love was about finding that unique individual who was just right for me. What I didn't understand was that in falling in love I would also discover who I really was. In the movie, *Sleepless in Seattle*, Tom Hanks describes taking his wife's hand for the first time and says that it was like 'coming home, yet it was to no home I had ever known before.' Learning to know our self and learning to be our self is like coming home. It is the secret to finding fulfilment in a relationship, in work, and in parenting. A good marriage makes this endeavour so much easier. A bad marriage makes it almost impossible.

Driving Alone

The last thing that I expected when I set out on my parenting journey was that there would come a time when I would travel that road alone as a separated and then divorced parent. I was committed, albeit innocently, to my marriage and my family, and believed that any problem could be worked out. I am not sure that I believe that anymore. Without a willingness on the part of both individuals to work hard, there is a limit to what can be reformed and healed.

A large number of single parents have come to realize that as arduous as single parenting is, it is often easier than parenting in a relationship that is plagued by continual criticism, anger, abuse, uncertainty, and above all, a lack of love. I think I would agree. I never imagined that I would be a single dad with the custody of my two sons, but it happened. Once I recovered from the shock, I did what most people do; I gave it my best and tried to move on.

Right from the start, I realized that if I were going to be doing all the driving, I wouldn't get any breaks. I had to pace myself and simplify routines. My two sons were fairly young at the time, five and nine, and fortunately for me they went to the same school that I taught in. We drove to and from school together, which made things simple, especially when someone was ill or if school opened late. With parenting, especially with single parenting, simple is good.

With all of the uncertainty that surrounds separation and divorce, I wanted to provide my sons with predictability and so I quickly committed to a regular schedule. On Mondays we came home right after school and did the laundry. On Wednesdays we went food shopping together. On Friday afternoons we always did something special — a hike or a visit to a friend's house. This simple schedule helped me take care of my children's basic needs and enabled me to provide them with a strong sense of familiarity and security. It also left some much-needed unscheduled time.

Being a single parent places inordinate demands on a person. It requires that we play all of the roles for our children. We are the cook, the cleaning person, the health care provider, the tutor, the playmate, and more. Though each of these jobs is important and many are intrinsically rewarding, doing all of them continually in a cheerful manner is not humanly possible. In order to survive as a single father, I had to set realistic goals, and that meant that some compromises had to be made.

When it came to dinner, quick and easy was important, but so was eating at home. I learned that there was a vast array of reasonable meals that can be cooked easily. Pasta with cheese, pasta with white sauce, pasta with meat and tomato sauce, pasta with oil and garlic became staples in our family diet. I went a little heavy on the carbs, but we survived.

My laundry got sorted creatively and our house was clean, but by no means spotless. I didn't drive myself crazy. I believed that what mattered most, given the age of my children, was my mood. If I felt hopeful and on top of things, those positive feelings were conveyed to my boys and reassured them. To this day, my sons remember those times with a certain fondness. They joke about the meals we ate and how predictable and how bad my packed lunches were. Looking back, it seems like we were able to make the best of a rough stretch of road.

Walking the Fine Line

When it comes to discipline, single parenting presents tough challenges. It calls on individuals to blend opposites consciously — to be both the comforter and the enforcer at the same time. That can be hard.

Most working parents make life work by creating a tenuous web of arrangements that are held precariously in place. This is especially true for single parents. It is easy to imagine the difficulties. Picture a particularly disastrous day.

For the second time in a week, your car won't start because the battery is weak. You had the car jump-started the other day and were hoping to replace the battery on the weekend, but the weather turned sharply colder last night and this morning the engine will not turn over. Then, you have to wait for more than an hour for the breakdown service and by the time they come, everyone is seriously late.

To make matters worse, your boss wants to see you when you arrive at work. He is upset that you were late again and 'perceives a troubling pattern of lateness,' citing this week's car problems and last week's orthodontist visit as only the latest in a series of belated arrivals. He even goes so far as to make ominous statements about job requirements and the need for professionals to take care of family responsibilities outside of work time.

But harder still is the phone message that is waiting for you when you stagger home at six-fifteen. It is from your son's teacher informing you that, for the second time this week, he arrived late without his homework and then proceeded to disrupt the class by making a joke of the situation. This is a sensitive issue and it provokes even greater discomfort. For weeks, you have felt that your twelve year old has been evasive about homework and unusually disrespectful. Now this too is coming to a head.

How we respond to a situation like this depends a lot on our personality. If we have a fiery nature, we may quickly fire off a series of staccato-like questions: 'What's going on? What did you do in class? What do you mean you didn't know there was a homework assignment?' After receiving a few evasive responses, all couched in a mood of seeming indifference to the seriousness of the situation, we move on to 'That's no excuse!' and 'You're grounded.'

This parent has become the enforcer, there doesn't seem to be any room for loving understanding. But what makes the situation even more problematic is that, by the end of the evening, this parent will probably feel guilty for over-reacting and will seek to mollify the situation.

On the opposite end of the spectrum is the parent whose reflex is to comfort. With a more passive and empathetic nature, different questions will be asked: Why don't you tell me what happened at school today? But why didn't you do your homework? Didn't you understand the assignment? Is something else bothering you? The playing field may be levelled further and the twelve year old addressed as an equal, foregoing the role of parental authority. 'You know I have a lot on my mind too. But I need you to take care of this. What do you say?'

And, of course, the child agrees to take care of it and in some cases, will. But in many instances, this approach simply enables a child to do the same thing again.

What is clear to me is that neither approach works all by itself. Single parents need to blend the two approaches continually in each encounter, offering understanding and comfort. They must be willing to ask tough questions and to live with discomfort at the end of a hard day. This takes a great deal of inner strength.

As a single parent, it is easy to lose perspective. For this reason, we need a support system, friends and relatives in whom we can confide — individuals who care enough to listen, but also care enough to speak the hard truth and tell us what we may not want to hear.

Driving alone certainly has its disadvantages. If, given our life situation, we become single parents, then we must find a way to provide our family with the kind of support that is more easily available in co-parenting situations. This means that we may have to work harder to provide the basics. But it also means that when we find our bearings and get accustomed to driving alone, we can take our children anywhere we choose, knowing it is up to us to select our route across this beautiful country.

CHAPTER SEVEN

Parenting as a Path of Inner Development

> The greatest single thing that you can do for your children is to work on yourself.
>
> — CLAIRE BLATCHFORD, *Turning*

From the start, 'The Changing Face of Parenting' seemed like the perfect title for the conference that our organization, the Nova Institute, holds each year near Washington D.C. Over time, I have learned that this title fits in more ways than I could have imagined. The name underscores how much parents' roles have changed in recent years and how both mothers and fathers are being placed in unprecedented situations. Unlike in times past, many families have both parents working, often with mums who travel for business, and sometimes with dads who work from home. Most parents can't look to the past and the way they were raised for examples of how to handle the complex and demanding circumstances that they find themselves in regularly. The face of parenting certainly has changed.

The first year that we held our conference, we had the images of comedy and tragedy on the cover of our brochure. These pictures served as an imaginative reminder of another aspect of parenting's continually changing face, how parenting both delights and disappoints us, bringing with it a full measure of joy and sorrow.

Recently, I discovered a third way in which 'The Changing Face of Parenting' is an apt title. While I was cleaning up some old photographs, I came upon a picture of myself holding my oldest son when he was a year old. He is now thirty-one and has a family of his own. One look at this photo of me as a young dad showed in a flash parenting's changing face and how the years of parenting re-shape us.

One other understanding that is conveyed by this title is that parenting, like all life affirming endeavours, will change us significantly on an inner level, transforming us in wonderful ways. On the long journey of childhood, parents will develop a wide array of positive attributes like selflessness, perseverance, patience, empathy, and more. Our work as parents will support and assist these changes.

Parenting is a path of development and it will call on us to change in deep and lasting ways.

> Self-development takes place at different speeds and on different levels. There are quick changes that occur on a superficial level. These readily noticeable changes involve alterations in thoughts and ideas. These changes come quickly, but they only scratch the surface. Their value is limited; it is simply too easy to talk a good game. Slow change is what we're after, and that occurs on a deeper level. It requires breaking long-held habits. These changes go unnoticed as we go about our business, and then after much work, we are surprised one day to find that we have changed. We have taken our . . . [parenting] to the next level.[21]

Parenting will reshape us in three distinct ways: physically, emotionally, and mentally. By far, the most striking physical sacrifices made on behalf of our children are made by mothers before their children are even born. From the early weeks of pregnancy, a mother's physical state is transformed for the sake of a new child. It starts with morning sickness and fatigue as a mother's physical substance begins to become her child's physical substance. These first physical gifts culminate with birth itself where a mother's physical exertion and pain usher this new life into the world.

Needless to say, mothers' physical sacrifices do not end with birth. Those first nights of a child's life extract another toll. Nursing mothers give up their sleep, the very thing that sustains and replenishes physical strength, so they can feed their children the food that their own bodies provide.

Surely the gift of a child is as wonderful as any aspect of human existence, a veritable miracle visited on us. Newborns delight and sustain, but truth be told, when children thrive, it is by virtue of loving sacrifice. Any parent of a young child, or better still, a parent of young children, can stop at nearly any moment and feel all the places where their body has made this sacrifice. Feet ache from standing all day; backs twinge from lifting and carrying children or bending repeatedly to pick up their things; and hands are often chapped and cracked from cleaning clothes, changing nappies and washing dishes.

The physical sacrifices we make on behalf of our children take place on many other levels as well. As parents, we also give up many of the things we want to do. When I reflect on my life in ancient times, B.C. (before children), I recall the types of exhilarating activities that captivated me. Travelling in Europe or high country hiking in the Rockies filled me with anticipation and excitement.

But as parents of young children, we often find that excitement eludes us. Advertisers know this. That is why they select adventurous, exciting names for SUVs — the Sequoia, the Trailblazer, the Tahoe, the Explorer, and the Expedition. These are names designed to make us feel that even a ride to the shop for nappies or milk can be an adventure, but of course we know better.

I remember as a young father planning the first vacation that we would take as a family when my oldest son was a year old. I had finished my first year of teaching and arrived at June with a clear sense that we should all get away. So, I arranged a ten-day camping trip to the Outer Banks of North Carolina, where I imagined our family would relax and be renewed by the ocean and the sun and the romantic glow of the Hatteras Lighthouse.

As conscientious (but naïve) parents, we collected the necessary camping equipment. We bought a large tent with a divider so that our child could have a quiet, separate place to sleep. We packed a portable crib, nappies, a pushchair, a cooking stove, and plenty of sun screen for our son — everything we could imagine that good parents would bring. How we fit all this in and on top of our VW Beetle remains a mystery to me. But we did and we made it to the tip of Cape Hatteras in time to set up our tent and make dinner and put our son to sleep.

On that first evening, one of those sudden thunderstorms so common to the Outer Banks rolled in off Pamlico Sound. The wind blew ferociously and lightning pierced the sky above the campground. Within minutes, the brand new tent collapsed in the pouring rain and my wife and I and our young child sought refuge in the VW where the three of us spent the night in very close quarters. Ours was the only tent on the whole campground that blew down.

Believe it or not, the trip got worse. When the weather cleared the next day, we found that the early summer sun rose magnificently out of the ocean and bathed the Outer Banks and our campground in light starting around 5:30 A.M. Daybreak woke our son with a start and the day began much too early. Later, when we returned from the beach for lunch and a little shade, we found construction crews working on our loop of the campground, building new tent platforms and making any quiet nap time an impossibility. By 9:00 at night, when the dust and dusk had finally settled, we had had more than the usual amounts of sun and sea. Within three days, I had sun stroke. (We had been diligent in putting sun screen on my wife and our son as they were both fair haired and fair skinned, but not on me.) Mercifully, the trip ended early.

I have always been a decent student and so obvious lessons aren't lost on me. I learned then, that now that I was a parent, my idea of vacation was going to need to change. However, it wasn't just my sense of vacation that needed adjusting. I also had to change what I thought were appropriate weekend activities. Activities of my choosing, like long bike trips and extended hikes, were soon deleted from the list of possibilities and replaced by short, tame trips to parks and botanical gardens. As I became an experienced parent, I came to see that modest walks (and carries) with abundant snacks were the most practical way to get outdoors for an enjoyable time in nature and still be back home in time for lunch and a nap. The kinds of things that I liked to do before I had children no longer seemed practical or appropriate.

I recently received an email from a young dad in New York describing how he had been lying on the couch exhausted after a hard day at work when his two-year-old son came into the room calling him, 'Come on, Daddy.' The father wrote, 'As he was calling me, I was thinking about how I could make things special for him and start this second important part of my workday in the right way. I jumped up and found the energy. I want to make every day something to be excited about and always to appreciate each moment.'

This is a fine example of good parenting, the kind of selflessness that will be developed in us as parents. As mothers and as fathers, we will be asked to set aside what we want to do and instead do what is best for our children and for our family. These are the sacrifices that we will be asked to make repeatedly, and with each passing year we will grow markedly different from the people we were before we had children.

Another place where we will be called on to change is in our emotional life. The kinds of feelings that passed through our soul and delighted us before we had children will slowly be replaced. Spontaneity, the capricious thought that we can just postpone dinner and go out for a long walk at sunset, will be purged by sobering visions of crying, cranky children with low blood sugar. Adventure, in the form of a ride on backcountry roads with no destination in mind, will be purged by anticipated shouts of 'Are we there yet?' and 'I have to go to the bathroom.' And even Romance, the expectation that this night may hold something magical, can also slip away over time as the demands of two full-time jobs — working and parenting — tire us out excessively and the need for a good night's sleep supplants our passion.

These once alluring possibilities will be replaced by other moods and other feelings. We will learn to weather disappointment with equanimity as parties and dinners get postponed or cancelled because of sore throats and ear infections. We will learn empathy through our children's disappointments and gratitude for their important accomplishments and for those wonderful days when all seems right. We will acquire patience, hopefulness, dedication, and selfless devotion, all characteristics of saints and sages. And hopefully, we will even learn to recapture spontaneity and romance in the midst of family responsibilities.

And lastly we will be called on to rework our thinking, to make it clear, defined, and strong. In the last phase of childhood, the teenage years, our children will demand that we support our parenting beliefs with lucid arguments and clearly stated rationales. Our teenagers will examine our values the way lawyers examine contracts and tax laws, looking for weaknesses, inconsistencies, and loopholes. We will be cross-examined at the dinner table, recalled as witnesses early in the morning, and asked to make depositions in front of friends and family, all in the presence of a relentless prosecution and a less-than-friendly jury. We will be asked to be clear, cogent, consistent, and tireless in the defence of the simple things that we are trying to uphold on behalf of our children. It will truly be a trial, and if we have more than one teenager, we will have to face a team of expert prosecutors.

Our thinking will be questioned and many of our most important beliefs will be resisted. There will be times when it will seem as though none of our values will have got through, but that will not be the case. We will be able to convey to our children the essential things that we believe. Our deeply held values will be transferred to our children if we communicate them through our actions by walking the talk and by expressing those values in warm and caring ways.

My son, Josh, was a strong-minded individual who resisted our parenting beliefs as adamantly as any child. One family practice that he found extremely unpleasant was our limited viewing of television, especially on school nights when we rarely watched at all. One day when he was around sixteen, he announced at the dinner table that when he lived on his own, he was going to have several television sets in his house, maybe one in each room, and he was going to subscribe to a large package of cable channels so he could watch Home Team Sports, ESPN I, ESPN II, Fox Sports and more.

I remember smiling at him and telling him that that was great. I knew he liked TV and he liked sports and I imagined that one day he would be able to watch those events to his heart's content. And then I added, 'But we just aren't going to do that here. We think that if the TV is on you won't read and reading is important. When you live on your own you will be able to watch as much television as you want. But while you are still at home, that's not going to happen.'

'That's ridiculous,' he replied exasperated. 'You guys are so weird.'

A few months ago, I got a call from Josh. He is now 27 years old and living on his own. He began the conversation by saying, 'I don't know what's wrong with me.'

'What's the matter?' I replied.

'I've read two books in the last month. You've really gotten to me.'

Our teenagers should resist our values. It is an important part of their development and the way in which they begin the life-long process of learning to think for themselves. But the important lessons that will be learned in this process are not necessarily the ones that we communicate in our defence, but rather the ones that are expressed indirectly. If our willingness to listen to our children's point of view promotes discussion, if our openness enables us to receive criticism without tightening our defences, we will convey to our children the most important lesson of all — that we respect both them and ourselves. That is perhaps the most valuable lesson we can give.

Parenting will ask so much of us. In fact, it will often ask more of us than we have to give. For that reason, we must remember that we can't parent alone. All parents, couples as well as single parents, need the support of a larger parenting community. We used to have this support with extended families, with grandparents, uncles, aunts, and cousins nearby, but that is rarely the case today. Something new must now be added. Parents today need to have supportive parenting networks, either through conferences, through local parenting organizations, through playgroups, or simply in informal neighbourhood gatherings at the playground.

In speaking and listening to other parents, we realize first and foremost that our challenging parenting situations are not unique. Our parenting dilemmas are more universal than particular. When we become aware of this, our burdens are lessened because we see that this is not just our problem or simply our fault.

When we converse with other parents, we begin to see that not only do we have common challenges, but we also can have common strategies. These strategies are based on a comprehensive approach for establishing sound, caring discipline, an approach that evolves during the three stages of our parenting journey from coast to coast.

But most of all, any sound parenting strategy must be based on the essential and inescapable principle that was best expressed by John Gardner — 'Our disciplinary influence upon children . . . is strongest when it works as the reflex of successful self-discipline.'[22] Although challenging, this premise is unavoidable. If we want our children to change for the better, we must be willing to change ourselves. This is a fundamental principle for effective parenting. Parents must be willing to take on the challenging work of changing themselves for the sake of their children. This is a profound undertaking.

Parenting is definitely a self-help proposition. But as has been noted, parenting also has a mysterious and paradoxical quality. There will invariably be times when we see that the antithesis of this understanding is just as true, that our best efforts at self-improvement don't really help at all. These moments come when we realize that the most important lessons are the hardest ones to learn or to teach. Our patience is limited, as is our aptitude for showing our children how to have empathy for others or interest in the world. Harder still is the realization that, try as we might, we are often unable to overcome the very characteristics in ourselves that give rise to the behaviours that we find most problematic in our children. Whether it is anger, criticism, or insensitivity, our faults linger and are passed on like some resistant bacterial strain, immune to our best efforts at eradication.

Here too, we should remember that we don't parent alone. For those parents who believe in a divine presence, something transcendent, wiser, and more potent than our human world, there is one more place to turn for help.

Several years before he died, my father came upon his family's Bible. In it he found a photograph of himself as a boy. His mother had used it to mark her place. What caught my father's attention was how the white border of the photo was all smudged with fingerprints. As he looked at the smudges, he understood that his mother had held this picture in her hands when she said her prayers. He was, by his own admission, a difficult child who had caused his mother to worry. She was simply asking for help.

Our various spiritual beliefs are like the facets of a jewel. Each reflects a unique side of a single universal truth. Whether we are Hindu, Muslim, Native American, Christian, or Jew, there exists an overriding sense that we are not alone. We have an intuitive perception, some inkling that there is a spiritual world that touches our human world, and when it does, it lights our way and helps us to see a little more clearly. When we need help urgently, we would do well to turn our hearts to a greater source of patience, love, and understanding and ask for help. I can't imagine any undertaking that would merit and elicit divine assistance more than parenting.

For some parents this request starts with a prayerful reminder at the outset of each morning of the important parenting work they have to do. For other parents it is the last thing they think about before they go to sleep. But in either case, the important thing is that we remember that help is there.

The Answer Is Often Closer Than We Think

What we love will speak to us.

— GEORGE WASHINGTON CARVER

I love splitting wood. I love the sound the maul makes, the smell of oak, the exercise, the visits from the neighbours, and all of the future fires stacked neatly, drying in the wood shed. Recently, I had a large pile of wood dumped on our front lawn. It was my job to split the stumps into firewood before all of the grass died, so I got right to work. Whenever I have to split large amounts of wood, I invariably start with the easiest pieces, those round thick sections of branch and trunk that are straight grained and straight forward.

This approach works very well until I near the end of the job. Then my enthusiasm fades because I am left with a pile made up entirely of the most intractable, gnarly pieces of wood.

With this last load of wood, I used the same process, working with the easier ones first, until I eventually moved on to the difficult pieces with crotches, branches, and knots. When I did, a significant breakthrough occurred. Each time I came to a piece of wood that seemed impossible to split, a thought would occur to me. 'What if you turned this gnarly piece over and tried to split it from the other side; would it split more easily?' Sure enough, it did. And then I thought. 'What if you put your wedge between these two inseparable branches?' The stump with the divided crotch immediately split right down the middle. In the end, I was left feeling that the wood itself was instructing me. Through my complete involvement and attention to this activity, I was approaching unity. The wood and I were almost one.

A couple of years ago I had a similar experience coaching baseball. To many people, baseball seems like a simple, uneventful, even boring game. I have never seen it that way. As a high school coach, I was often awed by the nuances and complexities of the sport. In crucial situations, for instance, with runners on first and third and less than two out, the possibilities seemed limitless and overwhelming. 'Do you play the infield back, or in, or at double-play depth?' 'What if they bunt or steal or both?' Often, I felt that I was a step behind the other team and its coach, struggling to keep pace. Fortunately, I realized one day that if I set my mind at rest and devoted myself to watching the game, I often came to know exactly what was going to happen and what, if anything, I should do. As I approached unity with the game I loved, it instructed me as well.

I believe it is the same with our parenting. When we are deeply attentive to our children, having set aside our frustration and worry, we approach oneness. Then what is deepest in our children can guide us and make our work easier and more effective. This is just the kind of help we need.

At its heart, parenting is supported by the promise that even when our best efforts fail, we can turn to a higher source to help us with this most important work. The guidance we need will come quietly and inconspicuously when we devote our loving attention to the children in our care.

Alaska and Hawaii

Parenting the Young Adult

> We shall not cease from exploration
> And the end of all our exploring
> Will be to arrive where we started
> And know the place for the first time.

— T.S. ELIOT

In the same way that the United States does not end with California, our parenting journey does not really end when our children graduate from college or begin their first job. I had a reminder of this several weeks ago when one of my sons called with an important question. He had bought an engagement ring and was planning to propose to the young woman with whom he had been living and wanted to know what I thought.

Fortunately, we had just been camping with him and his girlfriend and having seen them together, I was not completely surprised by the news. The two of them seemed to get along so well. They had been together for nearly three years and their relationship was easy. They laughed often and were sensitive to each other's needs. This young woman seemed to love my son and he obviously felt the same.

I smiled when he told me about the ring and I let him know immediately how much we liked his girlfriend, how they seemed like a sweet couple, and how pleased we were to see how well they got along. What I didn't tell him was how much attention I paid to their relationship on the trip. Having been through a divorce, I always observe the ways in which couples interact and how they affect each other. This young woman clearly brought out his best and he seemed to do the same for her. This was, perhaps, the most encouraging sign of all.

On this attendant journey through childhood we come to know our children deeply — who they are, what they love to do and what buoys their spirit. This understanding becomes the basis for the ways in which we interact with them. Maintaining a conscious awareness of our children's best is an essential part of the work we do as a parent.

When our adult children ask for our help with the decisions that matter most in their lives, a reflection of their best is what we have to offer. Because we have observed them carefully and lovingly for years, we have a pretty good sense of who they are. This acquired knowledge is what we should use to help us choose our remarks in these important conversations.

On the recent trip with my son and his fiancée, I couldn't help but gather important information. As we cooked our meals and hiked the trails, I could see that my son and this young woman understood and appreciated each other. This made it easier for me to respond with certainty when he called to speak about the engagement ring, because most of the important questions had been answered just by seeing them together. I was able to be reassuring and supportive and let him know that I shared his joy. But when I hung up the phone, I realized I had not done my job as a parent. I hadn't directly asked him the most important question.

So I called him back and immediately he was nervous. 'What's wrong?' he said when he heard my voice. I had to tell him that I hadn't done my job. 'How's that?' he said. 'I didn't ask you the most important question,' I replied. 'I didn't ask you if you were sure.'

'Oh yes,' he said, 'I have been thinking about this for months. I love her so much.'

Not all of the conversations that we have with our children when they are adults will be as delicate and as life changing as this one. Regardless of the topic, our role remains the same. Our primary task is to help our children find their own answers.

The Quakers have a practice called The Clearness Committee.[23] It has been in use for over three hundred years and is based on the deep belief that we already have within us the guidance we need to answer our important questions. When someone is faced with a difficult decision, they gather five or six people for a Clearness Committee and then present these people with a description of the question or dilemma. The job of the committee members is quite different from what we commonly expect in similar situations. They are asked not to give any advice. Rather, they are asked to pose real questions — a real question being one to which they don't already know the answer. In this way, the individual who is the focus of the group's attention has the opportunity to answer these questions out loud and listen at length to her own thoughts, to understand their own mind, and then eventually to come to their own decision.

As parents of adult children our assignment is similar, if not exactly the same. The way in which we listen to our children and the questions we ask will provide an important opportunity for meta-cognitive reflection. This will enable our children to think about their thinking.

For each of our children this questioning process will be different. When we are blessed with more than one child, we are often struck by how dissimilar they are. Their gifts and challenges can be poles apart, eliciting and requiring an entirely different style of questioning.

A colleague of mine, reflecting on the ideas in this book, remarked that his two children were as different as Hawaii and Alaska. His daughter, he said, was like the Hawaiian Islands — affable, warm, inviting, and easy. His son, on the other hand, was like the Alaskan frontier-independent, strong-minded, not as intimate, a more unwelcoming and challenging environment.

Individual children embrace their independence differently. Some have inviting natures like the Hawaiian Islands. They make any visit easy. But others, like Alaska, keep us at a distance. They are strong and majestic, but somehow unapproachable. The role that we play in our children's adult lives will vary depending on the terrain. But what remains clear is that in order to be helpful to our children we will have to base our interactions on a deep understanding of who they are. Then, we will be able to find the right way (and the right time) to reflect back to them in moments of crisis or indecision a sense of their best self.

At those special moments when our children ask us to help them with important decisions, it is our job to serve as an informal clearness committee and to pose questions that enable them to better understand themselves. This is a challenging assignment because we are invested in the outcome. It is much harder to facilitate this kind of discernment for someone you know well. Yet, this familiarity is also an advantage. It enables us to pose illuminating questions, questions that shed light on the issues that are most important to our children.

For our Hawaiians, those questions can be asked at any time — on a walk, on the phone, or over a meal, and they likely will be received with conversation that is warm and inviting. But with our Alaskans, we may have to wait for a break in the weather, for a time when the winds cease and the roads are passable. If we are patient, we will find the right moment to pose the right question in the right way, without any sense of what we think the answer should be. Then, through our child's response to our question, we will receive a glimpse of this new terrain, the place that our children inhabit now that their journey through childhood has ended.

For parents, this part of the journey requires just as much self-discipline as we continually listen more and speak less. In this new relationship, we can circle the world as friends now, not just as parents and children. And with a little good fortune, we may eventually find ourselves back on the shores of Cape Hatteras or another barrier island celebrating the birth of a granddaughter or grandson.

As I watch Jonathan, my oldest son, parent, I am so pleased to see what a fine father he is — patient, loving, humorous, and still firm. I can see that he remembers this journey from his own childhood and there are definitely places he wants to visit again because the memories are sweet. There are also spots that he would just as soon avoid. He and his wife now plan the itinerary, pack the car, and do almost all of the driving. As grandparents, we get to go along for the ride and really enjoy the scenery.

Notes

1. T. Berry Brazelton and Alan Greenspan, *The Irreducible Needs of Children: What Every Child Must Have to Grow, Learn, and Flourish* (Cambridge, Mass: Merloyd Lawrence Books, 2002), p. 57.

2. Laura Sessions Stepp, 'Teaching Timidity to Our Kids,' *The Washington Post*, 8 Dec. 2002. Section F, p. 1.

3. Jack Petrash, *Covering Home: Lessons on the Art of Fathering from the Game of Baseball* (Beltsville: Gryphon House, 2000), pp. 15f.

4. Rudolf Steiner, *Education of the Child and Early Lectures in Education* (Hudson, NY: Anthroposophic Press, 1996), p. 18.

5. Ellyn Satter, *How to Get Your Kid to Eat But Not Too Much* (Palo Alto: Bull Publishing, 1987), pp. 171–75.

6. Daniel Goleman, *Emotional Intelligence: Why It Can Matter More Than IQ* (New York: Bantam Books,1995), p. xii.

7. Parker Palmer, *The Courage to Teach: Exploring The Inner Landscape Of A Teacher's Life* (San Francisco: Jossey — Bass, 1998), p. 62.

8. Brazelton and Greenspan, *The Irreducible Needs of Children*, p. 149.

9. Inda Shenenen, *The 7 O'Clock Bedtime: Early to Bed, Early to Rise, Makes a Child Healthy, Playful, and Wise* (New York: Regan Books, 2001), p. 49.

10. Billy Collins, 'On Turning Ten' from *The Art of Drowning* (University of Pittsburgh Press, 1995).

11. John Gardner, *Reflections on Discipline* (New York: Myrin Institute, 1960), p. 13.*

12. Wendy Mogel, *The Blessing of a Skinned Knee: Using Jewish Teachings to Raise Self — Reliant Children* (New York: Penguin Compass, 2001), p. 92.

13. John F. Gardner, *Reflections on Discipline*, pp. 10f.*

14. Scott Russell Sanders, *Hunting for Hope: A Father's Journeys* (New York: Beacon Press, 1998), pp. 4–8.

15. Jack Petrash, *Covering Home*, p. 97.

16. Sarah Brown, 'Just Talking is Not Enough,' *The Washington Post*, 28 September 2003. Section B, p. 7.

---

* John Gardner's essay, 'Reflections on Discipline', can be found in *Youth Longs to Know*, published by Anthroposophic Press, Hudson, New York.

17. Steven Covey, *7 Habits of Highly Effective Families* (New York: St. Martin's Griffin, 1997), pp. 137–39.

18. Dan Kindlon, *Too Much of a Good Thing: Raising Children of Character in an Indulgent Age* (New York: Hyperion, 2001), p. 177.

19. Dan Kindlon, *Too Much of a Good Thing*, p. 48.

20. E.F. Schumacher, *Small Is Beautiful: Economics As If People Mattered* (New York: Norton, 1993), p. 35.

21. Jack Petrash, *Covering Home*, p. 3.

22. John F. Gardner, *Reflections on Discipline*, p. 15.*

23. For more information on Clearness Committees, please see Parker J. Palmer's book: *A Hidden Wholeness: The Journey toward an Undivided Life*, (San Francisco: Jossey — Bass, 2004).

Understanding Waldorf Education

Teaching from the Inside Out

Jack Petrash

A jargon-free view of Waldorf education and its philosophy of a three-dimensional education.

Since their inception over eighty years ago Steiner-Waldof schools have offered a much-needed model for educational reform. The author provides a compelling, clearly-written picture of the key components of a Waldorf education, focusing especially on child learning experiences that develop thought, feeling and intentional, purposeful activity.

Ideal for parents and teachers, this book gives a common sense understanding of an education which answers modern needs in almost 900 schools across the world.

www.florisbooks.co.uk

Why Children Don't Listen

A Guide for Parents and Teachers

Monika Kiel-Hinrichsen

What can you do when a child just won't listen?

How we speak to each other is at the very heart of human relationships. Children are often much better than adults at reading between the lines and deciphering the messages we send through body language and tone of voice.

This is an invaluable handbook for parents and teachers on how to communicate better with children. It covers all aspects of talking to and, importantly, listening to children, including communication with children of different ages and understanding the wider situation in which the conversation is taking place.

The author translates the theory into practical, everyday solutions. There are useful exercises throughout, to help us communicate more successfully.

www.florisbooks.co.uk

A Guide to Child Health

Michaela Glöckler & Wolfgang Goebel

This acclaimed guide to children's physical, psychological and spiritual development is now available in a revised edition. Combining medical advice with issues of upbringing and education, this is a definitive guide for parents.

This book outlines the connection between education and healing, with all that this implies for the upbringing and good health of children. Medical, educational and religious questions often overlap, and in the search for the meaning of illness it is necessary to study the child as a whole — as body, soul and spirit.

The authors based their theory and practice on 17 years' experience in the children's out-patient department of the Herdecke Hospital in Germany, which is run along anthroposophical lines.

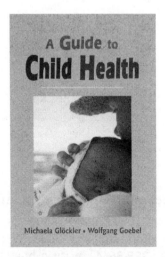

www.florisbooks.co.uk